Connecting with Colors

Discover the Transformational Synergy of
PERSONALITY COLOR STYLES
to Create Harmonious Relationships at Work, Home & Everywhere!

MARY ROBINSON REYNOLDS

HEART PRODUCTIONS & PUBLISHING

Heart Productions & Publishing

PO Box 56 • Newton Junction, NH 03859

Phone: 603-382-8848

MakeADifference.com

Table of Contents

Part I: The Colors of Life...5
    Chapter 1: Introduction 7
    Chapter 2: Using This Book...15
    Chapter 3: Instructions 17

Part II: Personality Color Styles..21
    Chapter 4: Intuitive Blues..23
    Chapter 5: Systematic Greens 37
    Chapter 6: Result-Oriented Reds 47
    Chapter 7: Don't Worry, Be Happy Yellows 57
    Chapter 8: Color Combos 67

Part III: Aligning Relationships 75
    Chapter 9: Connecting Colors 77
    Chapter 10: Matching & Mirroring 81
    Chapter 11: Practical Applications 87
    Chapter 12: A TurnAround Specialist 95

Part 1 The Colors of Life

Introduction

We could learn a lot from crayons:
Some are sharp, some are pretty, some are dull,
some have weird names and all are different colors...
but they all have to learn to live in the same box.

- Author Unknown

Connecting With Colors is not only about learning what makes our individual quirks and idiosyncracies valid, it's about learning how to embrace gently those problematic areas of our own and others' personality types. Individuals will learn from this that, ironically, our strengths are sometimes also our problematic areas.

Not only do we want to learn about ourselves, but we also need to consider the personality style of others that is most difficult for us to deal with and communicate with. When we learn about our own neurological wiring system and how it incorporates not only what we highly value, but how we think and integrate information, then we begin to understand why we are not on the same wavelength verbally and intellectually as someone who has entirely different values and thinking processes.

I have truly enjoyed field testing the information in this book with tens of thousands of people. I see this message as an educational conversation that can bring alignment between people everywhere. I know you'll find this information simple, straightforward and easy to use right away.

As I've traveled and spoken across the country, what I have found is that at the heart of every single person I've come in contact with, we all essentially want the same things: peace, love, harmony and good will.

It's really rather simple when you think about it. Peace, love, harmony and good will all come from one place—our hearts. I think you'll find that this light-hearted information brings new understanding, and with new understanding comes relief: we are all just human after all!

My introduction to personality styles began in 1994 when I was about to begin working as a seminar trainer for National Seminars Group (NSG) of Mission, KS.

It is one of the most beautiful compensations of this life hat no man can sincerely try to help another without helping himself.
—Ralph Waldo Emerson

That's when I studied the presentation of one of the seasoned trainers during a seminar entitled, *How To Deal With Difficult People.*

I loved an opening he used:

Do you work with a difficult person?

Do you live with a difficult person?

Are **you** the difficult person**?**

We each took a personality test in our workbooks and then the speaker began his humorous interpretation of each of the styles. This particular assessment was created by Virginia Satir and it included personalities styles labeled: *Blamer, Placater, Computer, Distracter* and *Leveler.*

The speaker had the entire audience laughing until they cried. He had me laughing too, at first, but then I gradually became more and more agitated about what I understood my husband's style to be. By the time I got home that night, I was so upset about my husband's personality style that it launched us into another round of our same old, drag-out argument. Both of us ended up being upset, exhausted and needing a "time out" to our separate corners of the house.

I had taken other personality assessments before, like *Myers-Briggs.* It was very extensive, but actually too thorough and complicated for a "keep it simple" person like me. I remembered nothing, and I didn't integrate anything from it that I could readily apply. Many years after, I found myself in a position where I would be training personality styles using the *Virginia Satir Assessment.* Her instrument was in every one of the workbooks I would be using to conduct seminars: *Dealing with Difficult People Seminar, Leadership Seminar, Powerful Communications for Women Seminar* and *Team Building Seminar.*

That night, in my corner of the house, I made a **decision.** Once again, the power of the label and the inflammatory effects on the person receiving the "label" offered me the opportunity to turn sarcastic and demoralizing labels into descriptions that were empowering and transformative.

As I designed my personal interpretation of the different personality styles, I simply turned the information around.

I re-labeled her descriptions using very specific, affirmative language, adding a light, humorous spin so people would be able to feel the relief of a new understanding of themselves and others!

Nothing is anything until you call it.

If you call something a failure, then your experience of it will be failure. If you call something a success, then your experience is success. It's all in how you decide to think about it and what you decide to call it.

Early in my travel schedule for NSG, I met another author who had developed a personality style program using the colors: Red, Blue, White and Yellow. His interpretation of the colors categorized Reds as the annoying bossy types; Blues as moody artists; whites as unmotivated layabouts; and Yellows as party animals. When I visited him for further discussion, he indicated that it was his belief that you are born a certain color and it's your life's work to "deal with it." His book and program has helped people, and yet, it just did not fit with my sensitivity toward de-energizing labeling.

As I look back at it today, I have concluded that, over the past thirty years, we have been advancing tremendously in healing generational legacies of attitudinal and verbal pain in our relationships. What was once considered acceptable *languaging* in our society is now being addressed: physical and emotional abuse, neglect, and what is (or is not) politically correct.

Unnecessary sarcasm and condescending labeling is now drawing the attention of a growing number of people seeking greater civility and harmony in all of our interactions: political, religious, and social. We are also seeing this transformational trend being carried into television shows like ABC's Primetime "What Would You Do?"

Language and labeling are so important when dealing with others. As well, they allow us to relax our own defenses long enough to be able to embrace areas that are, in fact, problematic for us.

Later that year, I was elected Director of Publications for the Oregon Chapter of the National Speakers Association (NSA). During our opening retreat, our NSA Chapter Liaison addressed our newly formed board of directors with a less abrasive version of personality styles using the four primary colors. From what I understood at the time, she had been given permission to use the color styles by a friend of hers who had developed the very basic descriptions for her business as a Color Analyst.

I thoroughly enjoyed her presentation and felt more alignment with how she described colors. Most importantly, I was not agitated with my husband's personality style that night! In fact, I started to see him with new eyes and a far greater degree of understanding and compassion. I found myself integrating the colors quickly into my thinking. I related this to everyone I was in conversation with, and discovered that previously difficult situations were now easing up dramatically.

A year later, she was invited back for our annual kick-off retreat and once again gave us her personality assessment to see if there had been any changes within our group. I found it quite interesting that last year's president-elect, who was now this year's president, went from a Yellow to a Red. Which suggests that we can most certainly change to accommodate whatever a situation demands of us. Not only can we fine-tune our ability to meet situational demands, but we can become virtually anybody we want to be.

Because it has made such a big difference in every conceivable area of my life, with her permission and blessings, I began to expand upon this basic information into every communication-based training I was doing.

I began adapting the colors to the more relevant and positive aspects of the S.E.L.F. Assessment which NSG had, in my second year, used as a replacement for Satir's assessment. I was able to pull some of my best and most humorous content that I had developed for understanding Color Styles and worked it into my own presentation.

I could now see how to make this topic very simple and **empowering** for people. I perused some of the leading personality assessments at that time, such as the D.I.S.C. assessment (Dominance, Influence, Steadiness, Compliance), in which I found descriptions of Dominant and Compliant to be too linear, subtly harsh and energetically inflammatory to one's psyche. Descriptions like these do not inspire people to rise up and be the best they can be.

So what I bring to you now is a culmination of my review of many assessments, combined with, importantly, what I have learned from very diverse audiences across the country. Speaking to over 20,000 people in the first two years alone gave me confirmation, changes and information to field test and develop a most effective tool for people to embrace and apply right away.

My audiences' feedback guided me in how to design a simple system that will help you define your predominant style and also help you see how your Secondary Color influences your Predominant, or Primary, Color. It's necessary that we understand and accept ourselves, so that we can understand and accept the idiosyncrasies of others.

The result of all my studies had an **immediate** and positive impact on my marriage, one that has continued to keep us aligned in our relationship ever since.

Back when I first started speaking, one of the frequent scenarios at the airport between my husband and me was the power struggle that began the second I'd step off the airplane! I'd come in after a long, intense week on the road with NSG— five cities a week, getting up at 6:00 a.m. to be on the floor setting up by 7:00 a.m. Presenting an all-day seminar, breaking down tables and books, packing up, then driving or flying to the next city. I'd get in at midnight, get up the next morning at 6:00 a.m. and do it all over again.

When I came in off the road I had only one thought: "Get me home!" I'd come off of that plane like a horse heading to the barn at night, with "get out of my way" stamped on my forehead.

Mr. Red encounters Ms. Green

This powerful urge clashed with my husband's predominant personality style. We'll discuss the different personality "colors" shortly, but let me say that a Green (me) and a Red (my husband) don't view the world in a similar way! Mr. Red would try to out-powerwalk me on the way to the parking garage. Being a Red and wanting to win, he'd play me like a game of chess, waiting 'til we got to the garage, then lowering the boom for the win—he knew where the car was parked, but I didn't!

Now that never really stops a Green, because we're certain we can do anything with the right system. So with my mind thinking very fast, I would calculate the most likely place he parked the car. At this point, his exasperation with me would heighten, because I didn't "need" him, and he'd say something like, "See, there can't be two leaders in this marriage," or he'd wait until I had sufficiently run around in circles long enough and say in a winning manner, "I know where the car is and you don't," and needless to say, an argument would ensue between us.

13

However, since I developed my four-color system of personality styles, I have discovered how quickly I can align myself with my husband, keeping our marriage harmonious and healthy. Now, whenever I arrive home from the airport and I'm locked into that Green mode, he will simply follow a few steps behind me (which is still a very, very hard thing for a Red to do) and he'll say to me,

"Oh, you're doing **that Green thing** again!"

So, now that he understands that his leadership capabilities are no longer being challenged, to him it's simply a Green thing. Are you starting to get an idea of where this is all going?

We live in a harsh, judgmental and quick-to-label society. This information not only makes practical sense, it is intended to soften those rough edges of our defense mechanisms. The defense mechanisms that kept us relatively safe as children may now be detrimental to the enjoyment of a kinder, more gentle life experience.

In giving you this information, which has been so life-changing and positively transformative for me, it is my intention that you have compassion with yourself and for those people in your life with whom you've been struggling. And with that said, we can begin.

Using This Book

If you are a professional development trainer or a person in a leadership position intending to take this training to your staff you will want to give this book to every person so they can follow along with your presentation and to invite constructive discussions. This is the kind of book they will keep on their desk as their number one "go to" reference. For best results, invest in our CWC UTrain Program with PowerPoint Slides and Script at:

ConnectingWithColors.com/UTrain

If you are reading this with the intention of improving your personal relationships, my recommendation to you is to read through the content several times thinking through how this applies directly to your existing relationships: peers, partners and family members.

To learn what your **Predominant Color Style** is, visit: www.ConnectingWithColors.com/PSP and take your FREE *Personality Style Profile*. Have everyone who is important to you take the test too!

When you complete this book, order copies for everyone on your team, in your family or within your circle of influence. The more people who get this information and expand their understanding of each other, the more relationships will be able to align.

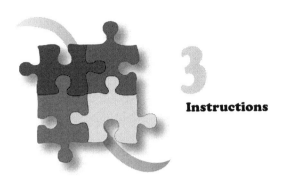

Instructions

F irst, complete the FREE *Personality Style Profile*–PSP at:

MakeADifference.com/PSP

Then read the chapters for each color. The following four chapters discuss each color's descriptions:

•Strengths   •Intellect   •Motto
•Problematic Area   •Little Quirk

Note that each color's strength is also its problematic area. Notice how you feel about the word 'problematic'? Here is an example of how a simple change in a word can change the attitudinal vibe we send out. Why is this? Because every descriptive word in our language has its own vibration, depending on the attitudinal spin we put on it. When you add an attitude to whatever that word means to us, then it becomes energy in motion. Communication breakdown is a direct result of what happens when we've called something right or wrong, good or bad, my way or the highway.

The word 'problematic' has an implication that it is solvable. In some personality assessments the term used in their descriptions has been the word 'weakness.' I stay away from that word because it suggests that something is inherently wrong with us. To many people it feels overwhelming and is therefore completely de-energizing and disabling.

'Problematic' on the other hand, just needs a solution. When we use the word 'problematic,' it sounds:

1. less severe

2. fixable or workable, and

3. less debilitating.

Therefore, our energy stays strong and flexible so we are much more empowered to own 100% responsibility for our lives and how we are literally teaching people how to treat us.

It is imperative that we all pay more attention now to how we "word" things, because as Rudyard Kipling said:

'Words...   **'**

are the most powerful drug known to mankind.

Be intentionally mindful of your language and the attitude it generates within you. Use this information as it applies to you and to the person or persons who most polarize you.

We all have a little bit of each of these colors in us. As you learn about each of the different styles, you will undoubtedly see yourself throughout all four colors. In learning how to communicate more effectively with finesse and ease, you must understand your Predominant Color as you relate and feel toward the other colors.

Your Predominant Color is where you instantaneously start interacting from, especially when under duress and/or what you may perceive as attack or adversity.

After you've read through the chapters on the colors, you will learn to apply the *Matching & Mirroring* technique that can improve all your interactions with people, and do so quickly.

About Your Secondary Colors

As I mentioned, you have a certain percentage of every color in you and you will see some part of yourself in every description.

Keep in mind as you are reading through the descriptions of each color, that your second highest color (your Secondary Color) may also be involved in your conversations right alongside your Primary Color.

When you see the description of your Predominant (or Primary) Color, you may think, "Well, that's not the way I do it." If that's the case, it's likely your Secondary Color is now jumping into the conversation, trying to control the situation (or to soften or strengthen) your Primary Color.

You will recognize yourself
as you read descriptions of your Secondary Color.

Discover what your personal colors are and learn how your colors interact with other, by completing the *Personality Style Profile*–PSP. You'll find it online at:

ConnectingWithColors.com/PSP

'There is no color better than any other.'

Part II Personality Color Styles

Blues are some of the nicest people on the planet! If you don't believe me, just ask a Blue. They will smile back at you with that "nice" Blue smile of theirs and say very proudly, "Yes, we definitely are the nicest people on the planet." There are smiles, and then there are "Blue" smiles. The line of their mouth is straight with just the right amount of upturn on each corner, about a 25° angle I would say, and that's what makes it such a nice smile and all Blues have one.

Blues love being **nice**. It is the highest quality they value. Blues really cherish people and they love working in an environment where there is the capacity for community and close knit, caring relationships.

To Blues, everything, and I do mean everything, is about relationships. Blues are in a relationship with you whether you meant to be in relationship with them or not. They just care. They care about you. They care about your family. They care about how everything is going. They really care and they want you to know that they care.

When Blues ask you how you are today, they are the one and only color who really does care. They actually want to know! It is not something superficial with them. They want the whole scoop from beginning to end. If there is something not right in your life, they want to know so they can help you make it better. If you've been hurt, they will be there for you in no uncertain terms.

You can count on a Blue. They are nurturers and wonderful caregivers. I've heard it said that, out of all of the colors, Blues give the best hugs, and my personal hug research happens to confirm this.

If a Blue asks you how you are today, and you say fine with a sad or weak tone in your voice, the Blue will have an arm around you so fast it will make your head spin. Blues will take you aside and tell you in a most soothing and caring voice, "Now, you tell me exactly what's going on. I can feel you're not so fine after all honey. In fact, you look just awful! Now, you just tell me what's going on and I'll see if we can make it all better." And with that, a person has literally no resistance with a Blue. The tears will begin to flow, the anger spouts in between sobs before you even know what's happening. You will confide your entire life to a Blue, because they are so caring and trustworthy with your tender, broken heart and spirit.

Oh, yes, a Blue always knows, honey, they always know.

Which brings me to the next aspect of their strengths. Blues are empathic: highly intuitive and sensitive.

You may be wondering, "What's empathic mean?" An empathic, or empath, is someone who is extremely in tune to the emotions of those surrounding them. Because they are so sensitive, they are intuitive and compassionate people. They usually have an interest in a wide range of topics, and because of this they are often very skilled at several different things.

24

Because they are always thinking about other people, they are generally very interested in other cultures and wondering how other people live. They view these ideas with a very open mind and rather than thinking about how living such a way would be different than their way of living, they imagine what it's like for the people of that culture.

Blues... hardwired with a genuine desire to help.

One of the most important things to understand about Blues is that they are empathic listeners. What this means is that they can hear beyond the veil of what mere words are saying. When a person says, "I'm fine," he or she can hear whether the words are true representation of what's really going on for a person, or not.

This is due to the fact that they are hard-wired with a genuine desire to help other people in any way that they can. They are so dedicated to helping others that they will put their own needs aside so they are better able to help someone else.

That's why a person can't get by in the mornings with a simple "I'm fine." Blues know when you are happy or sad and when you have been good or bad. Kind of like Santa Claus! Because they are so generous and so giving, you can even be mean or inadvertently harsh to a Blue and they are totally forgiving once they understand what you've been going through.

Blues forgive more readily than the other colors because they know that there was a "reason" why you did what you did. They fervently believe that all we need to do is uncover that reason behind why you did what you did, for everything to be all right again.

Another strength of a Blue is that they love doing their work, and they just wish everyone would get along so they could get their own work done! They truly believe that all of the world's problems would be solved in an instant if everyone would just learn to be nice.

Blues love sequence and putting systems into place intelligently, beautifully and diligently. They prefer that what is being asked of them is logical, but if it's not, they will work hard to implement it anyway.

They are amazing when it comes to taking care of the emotional climate of an office or home and still have the capacity to remain focused on getting their work done. Blues tend to be the calm in the middle of office (or home) storms. They are seen by others as the one who is capable of keeping things on an even keel. But Blues will tell you that while they carry a calm exterior they may very well be having intense and conflicting emotions inside. Blues maintain that calm exterior in public longer than the other colors, but by no means miss the signals they give out when they are about to cut, run and hide. Blues have fears and needs too, so let's be conscientious and take them into consideration.

INTELLECT

Blues are intelligent, intuitive and are great knowledge seekers. They ask a lot of questions in order to have time to assess alternatives and problems. They do not like to be pressured into rapid action.

Blues have what I will refer to as inventive minds. If I were to give a Blue a Rubik's Cube, they would immediately want to take it apart to determine how it was put together and why it was made. They think inventively, specifically in terms of how and why.

If you have a Blue on your team, or you're married to a Blue, when you are presenting an idea that you think they ought to just go along with, you will find that nothing happens until they know, "Why?" and "How?" Followed by, "Why?" "Why?" " Why?" "Why?" Not that this is irritating to anybody! Blues just need to know the why and how before they will proceed.

It is also a Blue who will have the perfect solution to your problem or have the right self-help book to recommend for you to fix what they perceive is wrong with your life. They love to give advice and self-help books as gifts. They truly believe that knowledge is power and if you've just got the right amount of information, you're life would be better. This is because they are such avid knowledge seekers themselves. They are invested in continuously taking workshops, reading self-help books, listening to audios because they just want to understand how to make everyone's life better.

Perfect Solutions Offered Here!

Blues are also, entirely benefit oriented. As nice as they are, they will, if necessary dig their heels in if they don't see how something will benefit people, society and/or the world. Blues get very frustrated if they don't see and understand what the benefit is. So if you have a Blue on your team, you will find that they just don't budge easily when it comes to a group vote on something that you may think should be obvious.

This is extremely important information if you selling a product to a Blue, are married to a Blue or have a Blue on your team.

If the benefit is not clearly defined and understandable to a Blue, you will not get their buy-in. Some Blues can be very resistant to change for this reason alone.

27

The other three colors move at a faster decision making pace than the Blues, and they often assume that a Blue's silence is their agreement. Their silence may merely be their non-agreement so don't forge ahead until you've heard from them!

One time I was working with a client, and we were in agreement on my fee and the training I was going to do for her company and yet, three weeks after our confirmation of the date, she had still not signed the contract or issued payment to me.

In thinking through each of our conversations, I tried to figure out what was holding up her commitment, when I realized just how Blue she was and that I had not done anything to advance my relationship with her.

I immediately picked up the phone and called her to have a conversation for the sake of having a conversation with her. Because Blues are so relationship oriented it is also one of the benefits.

During our time together on the phone, I did not mention our upcoming training or the contract. To my surprise she stayed on the phone with me for nearly an hour. We talked about the relationship "stuff" that was of interest to her and had nothing to do with business.

As we both recognized that we needed to get back to work, and as I was saying my good-byes, out-of-the-Blue she followed by saying, "Oh by the way, I'll fax over the contract and initiate payment this afternoon."

A Blue's resistance to moving forward is usually very quiet, and they are more than patient about allowing you the time to come to your own realization that you do not have their agreement.

Because Blues are known for not rocking the boat this brings me to their...

MOTTO

BE NICE, DON'T MAKE WAVES AND SMILE AT ALL COSTS!

Now if you ask a Blue how "they" are today, the rules change here considerably because a Blue's "pat" answer is also fine!

It's okay for a Blue to not really be fine and not share, but it's not okay for you to not really be fine and not share. When Blues say they are fine it can be interpreted as:

F eelings

I nside

N ot

E xpressed

While this acronym applies to them, it applies to most people in our society who say that they are fine whether they are fine or not. Blues just happen to be highly inclined to keep the focus on others and away from themselves. This one issue alone can become their...

PROBLEMATIC AREA

Because Blues prefer being nice to being rude, inconsiderate, brash, flamboyant or just plan nasty – they are often told that "the problem with them is that they are just too nice and they let people walk all over them."

This is absolutely crazy-making to a Blue.

Saying something like this to a Blue solves nothing. It only succeeds in alienating yourself from their kind graces.

Trying to make a Blue, or anyone for that matter, feel bad for being nice when it's something that they deeply value is hurtful and harmful. Deep inside, Blues have no desire to change being nice, and yet, because of outside influences, can be deeply conflicted about this. This can increase their emotionality, not decrease it.

When addressing this problematic area, Blues will weep in my trainings when they are given this information. Since being little children, Blues have been told that they are just too nice and/or just too sensitive. They have been told repeatedly that they are making something out of nothing, and that they just need to buck up and get a tougher skin grown on.

When a Blue understands that their niceness, intuition and sensitivity is a strength they cry because it is such a relief. To be told that their perceptions of what was going on was not only accurate, but that what they were really trying to request of people was valid is truly empowering.

People who use bullying tactics to dominate and control others will be the first to tell the Blues that they are just too sensitive. All a Blue needs to do to neutralize the person who has done something hurtful is to say, "You are right, I AM sensitive and I still want you to stop hurting people in the way that I've observed."

[Notice, Blues, that you will not say that you are too sensitive. You will just own that your are most definitely sensitive to people being unnecessarily hurtful to others. Period!]

This type of situation has been problematic for Blues who have never been supported to know what they know, feel what they feel and want what they want.

It is problematic for a nice Blue to stand up to a very strong personality style, such as an extreme Red, who, by the very values of that style, really don't care like a Blue does. And because Blues are nice, sensitive to others needs and prefer to not rock the boat, they tend to be, indecisive!

The Story of Two Blues Going to Lunch

One Blue says to the other Blue,
"Where do you want to go?"

And the other Blue says,
"Oh, I don't care, you decide."
"No, you decide."
"No, you decide."
"Well, you're driving."
"Well, here's my car keys, you drive."
"No, you drive."
"No, you drive."

An hour later...

"So, where do you want to go?"
"I don't care, where do you want to go?"
"You decide."
"No, you decide."

Blues can be indecisive not only because they don't want to rock the boat, but because they really hate, hate, hate confrontation. If someone becomes angry with them, they will do all they can to make sure that the dispute is resolved very quickly and in the most peaceful manner possible. Their preference is to avoid confrontation altogether. They will literally leave a room where heated disagreements are taking place. You'll notice them there one minute, and then just about the time you need their wise input, they have left the room.

This is problematic for Blues for two reasons:

1. they are wise, knowledgeable and have something to offer that they did not stick around to offer, and

2. they need to learn that just because they are empathic and sensitive to the energy of a heated interaction, they can in fact master their own emotions, and in doing this, they can actually neutralize the situation by Matching & Mirroring (Chapter 10).

In fact, it's imperative that Blues learn to do this, because allowing yourself to have an avoidance reaction to conflict will eventually hurt your credibility and career advancement. With family members, an avoidance reaction means that you will not be teaching the members of your own family how to effectively master their emotions and remain in their own power. Avoidance in this area of your life will never improve relations; it will only magnify existing issues in need of healthy resolutions.

While on the one hand, Blues can be the calm in the middle of a storm, as in someone in urgent physical or emotional need. Then yes, Blues navigate the storm beautifully. If, however the storm is about conflict and confrontation, they will find themselves distressed, wanting to flee as fast as they can.

If you are a Blue who closes the door and refuses to have any conversation at all, realize that your avoidance accomplishes nothing and any compliance you may get out of it, will be short lived!

Certainly there is great wisdom, in "picking your fight," but I'm not talking about that. I'm talking about using a closed-door method as a way to manipulate, guilt or to give ultimatums. While these may appear to work initially, they are not empowering to yourself and are not going to bring you the long-term, harmonious agreements you and everyone else would prefer.

How do you become the master of your emotional state when things are getting intense and you are feeling overwhelmed by it all? In those moments when you feel like running, simply start saying this to yourself:

'I am the Master of my Emotional State'

Blues can get depressed, down or just plain "Blue," choosing to seclude themselves, even if just for a day, so they can get quiet with their thoughts. This may be because, empathically, they are taking on so many emotions that may or may not even be theirs, which can be very emotionally draining, so Blues often need some time to recharge.

Some Blues can be so extremely sensitive that they will often feel what is happening to other people more so than they will feel it if it were happening to them.

Because of this, they will sometimes ignore their own needs.

Because Blues are sensitive, it is important to make sure when you are teasing them, that you also check in with them to make sure that what they've understood is congruent with what you meant.

They will often find it hard to process when someone thanks them or gives them a compliment. They are much more likely to pay someone else a compliment than to accept one.

Why is this problematic? In the business world, not accepting a "thank you" or a compliment can be misconstrued as a lack of confidence and competence. The solution to this is to simply accept graciously and then close your mouth!

Blues can also be sensitive to those that they don't know. This means that after seeing violence on television especially to children or animals, it may be too hard for them to take and they may easily cry over it and seem to have a very hard time getting over it. The solution to this is to simply change channels! Taking on the tragedies of others serves no one, and certainly not you. You are the master of your emotional state. You can best serve others by living in an emotionally uplifted state because that is what will lead the way for them.

Blues naturally draw people to them, because other people can sense how sensitive and caring they are, whether they realize they are being drawn to them or not. This applies even to strangers, because Blues have a certain kindness, and others can see it.

Why is this problematic? It is only problematic if Blues overextend themselves and do not make time to renew themselves every day.

LITTLE QUIRK
'Don't Touch My Stuff!'

Now, every Blue knows what this means. This means that everything has a place, a specific place, and that's exactly where the Blues want it to stay. Blues always know when someone's been in their office or home. Why? Because something's been moved or touched. Oh yes, Blues can even tell when something's been touched! They can sense your energy and your fingerprints on their stuff.

Blues hate having their "stuff" touched. It's like a total personal violation to them. And while other forms of confrontation are difficult for them, they will be ever so powerfully moved to say something, very nicely I might add, about how you touched their stuff.

You might hear something like this from a Blue:

"You see this figurine, it's at a 45° angle! It's supposed to be at a 90° angle. You see, this is 45°, this 90°. Look, 45°, now 90°. I had it at a 90°. It's pleasing at 90°. It balances out the entire room when it's at a 90°. And this over here, it's suppose to be there. Why? Because it coordinates all three rooms together in such a way that can only be explained as heavenly, orderly and in total balance and serenity. And about the bath towels. You know I've asked you nicely not to use the towels in the bathroom. Why? Because they are for decoration and guests only, your towels are in the closet."

Blues would never say, "Because it just does." No, they think you should really care and you, like them, would want to have a full and complete explanation of why everything must remain in its exact place!

35

I once had a Red manager in a training, and right after this section on the Blues, he raised his hand and said, "Oh, now I think I understand why each and every time my wife and I have an argument, I run around the house tweaking all of her knickknacks!" Of course, I tried to appeal to his greater sensibilities to stop messing with her stuff—that is if he ever wanted to have sex again!

Here is an example of where, let's say, you are predominantly a Red and have Blue as your Secondary Color. Even though you experience yourself as a Red most of the time, you may just have this Blue quirk thing going on where if somebody touches your stuff, it really sets you off.

Keep in mind as you read through the different colors, how, when and where some of your secondary colors come into play for you.

That's it for the Blues. If you are a Blue, you can now relax and breathe. This wasn't so bad after all.

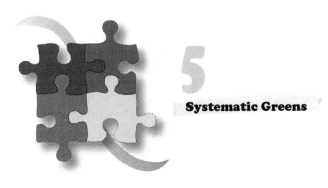

5

Systematic Greens

Greens must have a system.
And if there's not a system,
they're going to make one up!

Greens are highly functional and productive. They love, love, love to create systems that are logical and sequential. These systems are highly designed to be the ultimate in energy and time efficiency! Out of all the colors, the Greens are the only ones who literally can do ten things at the same time. There is another color that thinks they can, but trust me, they can't!

Greens love their lists, and they love the feeling of being prepared. This is why their systems are so important to them. If they do not see a systematic way to approach a project, they are unable to move forward until they do.

STRENGTHS

Greens have the ability to see the "big picture" long before any of the other colors. The other colors may still be discussing concepts, choices, breaking things down, having more exhaustive discussions, while the Green has already started on the project, because they see exactly what needs to happen, in a systematic order. They are already out the door getting to work on it. They are totally focused about getting the job done.

Greens are not as people-oriented as the Blues. They do like people, and they think the time for social interaction comes after they've completed their work. They, like the Reds, don't need people like the Blues and the Yellows. Greens and Reds are work-oriented, not people-oriented in the emotional ways that the Blues and Yellows are.

Also, in their ability to see the big picture, Greens often can see impending problems long before it has even occurred to anyone else. They are the one color that can literally turn "what if" ideas into creative systems and benefits. They are reserved, cautious and they make decisions only after careful systematized evaluation.

They are 'take-charge' people as far as any opportunities are concerned. That's why, when a team of people are gathering to make a decision, the Greens can be restless in wait of what they already know needs to happen.

Greens walk around with their noses slightly in the air; tilted up to about a 45° angle. The Blues think that the Greens are stuck up and uninvolved. This is not exactly true. Greens are simply busy, busy, busy – think, think, thinking! The Greens would never think of themselves as stuck up. They see themselves as seriously thinking about important stuff, stuff and more stuff.

They don't mean to ignore you.

They are so busy thinking that they simply did not see you as they passed you in the hall. Seriously, I know that to the Blues this seems impossible, because they care so much about greeting people in the hallways, but this is what is actually going on for Greens. Greens really don't see people in the hallways, they just don't!

So, while they may be momentarily uninvolved with you, they are involved in figuring something out for humanity at large.

INTELLECT

Greens have very systems-oriented, creative minds. They see the big picture, and they see it in flashes coming together like pieces of a puzzle which thrills them. They think very fast, they prefer to go very fast, many of them speak very fast, and it will be a Green who finishes your sentence, your paragraph, and your entire page of thought before you've even opened your mouth. Why? Because they already see where you're going with whatever you started to say, so why wait around for the entire conversation? To a Green, having to wait for you to finish your sentence is such a time constraint! They like to go, go, go. And to wait for this entire conversation with you to end, frankly, is costing them time on that ever-ticking internal clock of theirs.

Greens travel mentally to a place that I will refer to as The Zone! All Greens know where this place is. Oh, yeah! It is so mentally stimulating in the Zone! Just ask a Green. That's why it's so hard to get their attention. They love the Zone, and they love think, think, thinking in the Zone.

In fact, two Greens who find each other in the Zone—their families never see them again!

Greens are also very positive people. They believe that everything is possible—everything! All that is really needed to any impossible situation is the right system, and they are going to be the ones to think one up. They love thinking up possibilities, especially when there appears to be none. They know that all that's required, really, is just the right system and all will be well and on its way to completion.

Completion! Oh, what an orgasmic word that is to Greens. They love the feeling of a completed project. Ohhh... how stimulating it all is to see something to fruition. They love the creative process of designing a system, they love implementing their own system (thus, usually denying the Blues of their work) and they love, love, love the completed project. They love to stand back and admire their own work. It is the ultimate high to a Green.

No Time For Negatives!

Back to being positive: Greens are so positive that they can be a little hard to take sometimes, especially to the colors that consider themselves more realistic and grounded in what they believe negative appearances are really saying. And the Greens just hate this. They absolutely have no time for negatives, because this feels to them like they are not only being slowed down, but being totally dragged down energetically. They feel it interferes with their ability to stay in the Zone, where everything is just a design module away from fixing anything and everything.

As I mentioned, Greens have no time for negativity, but watch out for a Green without a nap! Well, let's just say that negative energy is nothing compared to an irritable Green who has been working non-stop on a project for too many days without adequate rest. Which, by the way, is natural for a Green: to not stop for days on end.

Why? Because they are driven by being in the Zone, where the flow of creative ideas comes together in a sequential system that can then be implemented.

In the Zone, Greens have no concept of time or space, let alone people. It feels like things happen simultaneously in the Zone and, most importantly, they can multi-task their brains out!

What a mental trip this is for them. They don't want anybody or anything in their way that could possibly interrupt their intense focus. In other words, when a Green is in the Zone, leave them alone.

MOTTO

GET OUT OF MY WAY!

Greens remind me of little roadrunners. Beep-beep. Zip, zip, zip, zooooommmmm! Off they go. If you have a Green on your team, you will notice that they take off and go to work on a project before any agreement has been reached. Which, of course brings us to their...

PROBLEMATIC AREA

Greens actually have two problematic areas. Both are related, as you probably guessed, to the amount of time they prefer to spend in the Zone!

Delegating: Greens are not very good at delegating. Why you say? Because they hate handing off the system that they just created. Yes, it's true, they'd rather do it themselves. They believe that it would just take too much work and, most importantly, too much time to hand it off or delegate. Besides, no one can do it as well as they can after all, so why bother asking? (Oh, I guess there may be some truth to the Blues perception that Greens are a little stuck up after all!)

Greens work diligently, not really thinking about rewards, and while it is a strength, this is also problematic in being a collaborative team member, which in turn impacts their career advancement.

Not only can they literally do ten things all at the same time, they make it look easy! Therefore, people have no idea how much work a Green really does, and they rarely receive recognition. Because of this, other people on their teams may perceive the Greens as not being cooperative team players.

Greens have a bit of an attitude about this, because they don't see anybody stepping up and pitching in. The road goes both ways, and the Greens may have only been looking at it from their perspective. Meaning that, people won't step up because, frankly, why should they? Not everybody is as devoted to doing work as the Greens are.

Greens, out of all of the colors, have the highest tendency to be workaholics and entrepreneurs, because they can spend extensive amounts of time without human interaction. Many have a very challenging time delegating, slowing down and communicating about the specifics of a project. They just don't know when to stop jumping back in and taking the projects back, just because someone isn't doing it 1) fast enough, or 2) utilizing the specific system the Green designed for them to use.

Greens struggle to tolerate any variation on a theme or system once it's been designed. That's why it can be problematic for them to work synergistically with a team if they don't decide to do something different about this.

Health and Energy Depletion:

OK Greens, you can figure this one out yourself. If you never look up, stop to take a breath, get a little human contact or delegate any work, then the likelihood that you are taking good care of yourself and your energy reserves is slim to none. The problem is that you will become burned out if you don't pay attention to this.

If you don't learn how to delegate constructively and start slowing down long enough to effectively train people on the various things that will work and won't work about your systems, how can you ever expect people to step up and want to work collaboratively with you?

You might want to consider not doing everything yourself, alone. Other people in this world need you to delegate and teach them how to create their own systems. Other people need to contribute and step up and give of their talents.

Delegate, Delegate!

While systematizing and undertaking impossible projects, making them possible is your gift and your talent, there are plenty of projects out there for everyone. Release your grip and give it away.

What could be beneficial about you being a martyr? Nothing, absolutely nothing. Which brings us to your other fear. Your other fear is that if you aren't busy with projects, then what will you do with yourself?

Designing systems for projects is and always has been your idea of fun and having a good time, and there's nothing problematic about this. The likelihood is that you have relationships and other creative interests that are not getting attended to. Yes, that means to really be as effective as you are driven to be, you must slow down and "be" with people.

Making time to come out of your work space and connect with people is an excellent way to rejuvenate. So, it's worth your life, your health and important relationships, to bring your mental attention into real time.

43

Dial down the roadrunner mental activity just a little bit, so you really can offer the benefits of your interests to the people you live with and work with.

LITTLE QUIRK

To anyone other than a Green, this might come as a surprise. But all Greens will agree that their little quirk is that they are highly, highly critical of themselves, internally. Inside a Green's mind is ongoing self-criticism. Because they love the creative endeavor of making systems, it is also equally important to them that everything be perfect. They are perfectionists in many ways. They are concerned with perfection each and every time, and they hate it that other people aren't as concerned as they are about things being just right.

This causes the Green additional stress to an already geared-up mental lifestyle of do, do, do, doing. This high level of self-criticism is not warranted, even though Greens have believed that it is.

Inside a Green's mind is ongoing self-criticism.

If you have feedback or criticism for a Green, this will help you understand why they don't receive it well. They have already chewed themselves out extensively for anything that was even a smidgen less than perfect.

When you offer your "feedback," their defenses go up because so much criticism has already been taking place in their minds, so they just don't want to hear any "feedback" from you, too. Is this beginning to make sense?

44

They've probably over-extended themselves in getting the project done, and then you think you have something to offer them. Certainly, it is not going to be received well by a Green at this point.

If you are dealing with Greens, back off and wait a while. Ask them what they think, and you'll find out what's going on in that head of theirs. Then you'll know how to proceed and collaborate on making additional improvements.

If you are the maxed out Green, then you need to take a nap and work on trusting your talents to be enough. I've heard it said that the Chinese intentionally weave one mistake into their rugs, because they believe that imperfection is perfection.

Finally, if you are a Green, and you are being highly critical with yourself, know that this is negative attitudinal energy, and it's bound to start attracting more of the same with other people. Oops! I know how much you prefer being positive, so maybe now you will be motivated to ease up on being so critical of yourself! Right?

Take a breath, ease up and let go your strong hold on the projects for which you have designed systems. Trust that it will get done. Why trust? Because things always get done!

Red's key desire is Results!

It doesn't matter what job position or title Reds have, they think they are the boss!

STRENGTHS

Reds generally make great leaders and delegators. They make great administrators because they have their fingers on the pulse all of the time. They are constantly checking people out to see exactly what talents they possess, and who can do what the fastest and most efficiently.

Reds know how to fix things that are broken or are not running correctly. They are take-charge people. They are strong-willed and intense. They make it their business to oversee work being done, and they make it their business to make sure it's being done right!

Reds know how to take ideas and call in the people who can put them in place. They can come into a crisis situation and assess what needs to happen to get things running again. They are quick to delegate and get people to work. They have no problem delegating like the Greens and Blues. As they see it, that's their job: delegating, of course!

They are bottom-line people who want accomplishments and achievements to be done **Now!**

Having leader mentality, they generally are not inclined to beating around the bush. They say it straight. They get to the point and don't waste any time.

Reds are an interesting bunch, because on the one hand, unlike Blues, they really don't care what people think about them, and on the other hand, they can be courteous with people in order to get things done.

They are totally results oriented. They love the feeling they get when they know that they can make things happen. They love stepping up and stepping forward. They love leading!

They love taking risks. Concrete calculated risks, that is. A Red will never proceed until they've evaluated something thoroughly. To other people who were not privy to the Red's exhaustive research, it may seem that they are quick to take risks, but they really aren't. They will do the numbers and do their due diligence before moving forward.

Reds love the challenge of the risk, and they love change.

INTELLECT

Reds love, love, love an intellectual challenge. They love change and variation. They get bored if things remain constant. They seek to be intellectually challenged and, because of this, they have a mind for leadership. They love checking out every detail.

Challenges— Bring 'em on!

They love researching a thing from every

conceivable angle, which drives Greens nuts, because Greens are ready to rock and roll and will resist how they perceive Reds are slowing them down. Blues see the logical explanation of the Red's extensive research, while you will see in the next chapter that Yellows really don't care one way or the other.

The Reds will go to great lengths and spend as much time as necessary to adequately analyze their findings. They like going through everything so thoroughly that they are absolutely certain that every conceivable angle has been sought out to assure a successful outcome.

They are sticklers for details that may seem small to the other colors, but quite possibly will become critical for the success of a project. They are numbers and statistics people.

They will spend the time it takes to go over everything two, three and four times to make sure that every task is appropriately delegated. Greens by this point are like holding a race horse in the starting gate, and not pulling the bell to start the race.

Reds are the Micro-Managers of the world!

If you haven't guessed by now, yes, Reds are the micro-managers of our world — or some would refer to them as intense! And most Reds would readily agree with this description.

Reds love, love, love using their minds to break things up into parts. That's why they are great when it comes to overseeing a system that needs to be put in place, and in delegating to those who they know can handle the work.

In any business environment, you will see more Reds in managerial and executive positions than any other color. Why? Because they can delegate, delegate, delegate and not be deterred (or thrown) by what other people think or don't think regarding their decisions.

If a person was not a Red coming in to higher-level management, the likelihood that they will need to dial-in some Red is pretty high. It's not to say that you won't see any of the other three colors in upper-level management, just not as many.

Generally, to be an effective leader, a person simply must find a way to integrate Red into their personality style to create the momentum needed to succeed.

Reds don't think fast like Greens, but they want everyone to do their work fast, like: **NOW, NOW, NOW, NOW.** When does a Red want it? NOW! Which leads me to their motto…

MOTTO #1

I WANT IT DONE RIGHT

I WANT IT DONE NOW, or…

I WANTED IT DONE, YESTERDAY!

Because they are Reds, they actually have a second motto. There is something everyone really needs to know about Reds. They are highly, and I do mean highly, competitive. So, whether you know you are in competition with a Red or not, it does not matter, because as soon as you enter the room, the game is on, and the Reds fully intend to win. So...

MOTTO #2

WINNING ISN'T EVERYTHING... IT'S THE ONLY THING!

As is true with all the colors, Strengths have a habit of becoming the color's:

PROBLEMATIC AREA

As high achievement-oriented and results-oriented as Reds are, their problematic area is listening! But there's a reason for this:

They don't have time, and they already knew the answer yesterday. So why listen!

As much as some Reds may want to minimize the importance of this, listening is actually highly problematic for Reds who intend to advance their careers and/or improve their personal lives. When Reds listen, they tend to listen to what they think is important rather than what is actually going on, or is important to the person speaking.

Reds could learn a lot from Blues' empathic listening abilities, being able to hear beyond what the words are saying.

Reds may think they are listening, but they tend to not really hear what is actually being said, offered or asked. If you ask a Red, "What shall I tell the customer about giving them a refund; yes or no?" the Red will give a dissertation about something that has nothing to do with the question and more importantly the answer that people are waiting for.

While Reds abhor small talk from others, especially if it interferes with work, they do not see imparting their extensive intellectual prowess as chit chat at all.

Let's face it, Reds enjoy their intellect and so they like hearing themselves talk! There is nothing wrong with sharing your vast intelligence on any subject. However, it may be problematic to those who have to listen to you. You can simply make a mental note to yourself, Reds, to notice if people have a glazed over look in their eyes. If they do, it's time to wrap it up and check in with them to see if you have adequately answered their question.

Time will either promote you or expose you. Each of the other three colors believes that is it important to be listened to and recognized as having something relevant to add, and Reds have a difficult time honoring this in other individuals.

When two Reds interact, the result is either 1) respect or 2) an ongoing battle of wills.

When a Red interacts with a Green, you have a battle of wills and power. A Red has a very strong competence power base because, like a Green, neither require the approval or input of others to feel confident to go forward. Whereas Blues' and Yellows' power base is so relationship-oriented —needing others' input before making a decision to just get started—Reds generally have very little patience with what appears to be a lack of fortitude. Reds really have no interest in small talk if it has nothing to do with getting down to the business at hand.

Unlike Blues, Reds really do enjoy the spotlight, will accept praise and acknowledgment quite easily. They have an expectation that, quite honestly, people who succeed should be recognized for their accomplishments.

Love that Spotlight!

Out of all the colors, the Blues can have the most difficulty with Reds, because they can be very harsh to the Blue sensitivities. Reds don't get what the big deal is! But if a Red is to become a great leader, then he or she needs to be more accommodating and inclusive with Blues. Blues can be your strongest advocates or the most irritating miniscule sliver in your foot.

Yellows and Reds are actually entertaining to watch together, because Reds are so intent on winning that they can't see how the Yellow is playing them — the Reds, of course, think that they are winning while the Yellows have won hours ago.

Clearly Reds have a tougher skin that's more deflective than any of the other three colors. Some would even say that they are quite insensitive. A Red would say, "Why is this problematic?" Exactly my point.

If you are to succeed, you must have a collaborative, synergistic team to succeed with. That means you must learn to soften some of your exterior Red edges so people will want to collaborate and cooperate.

While Greens are similar to Reds in that they really don't need approval or input, Greens are more concerned about what people think and any attitudinal vibe that comes their way.

Reds, are generally very self-confident and pumped up on who they are and what they are about so they really don't fear anyone or anything. In fact, if they do experience fear, they generally utilize this as the means to get even more competitive. They can increase their focus to laser quality when it comes to an intellectual challenge any difficult situation might pose.

Reds clearly are about the business of business, and they really don't see what the big deal is when it comes to relationships. "Just do your job and knock off the small talk," is basically how they see things.

They would rather take the longest route to their work space than walk by people in their office who might want to have a conversation or provide unsolicited input. Reds just don't get it intellectually. Their thinking is: "We are here to do a job, so let's do it! You want to have a chat, save it until after work! If you have relationship problems at home, leave it at the door when you come to work. Your personal problems don't belong here." This is a Red's entire mental construct, and they have no intention of changing their views on this, unless they can see how it is hurting their ability to succeed and/or get ahead. Which really gets Blues' knickers in a bunch! "How can you succeed without caring about people?" Blues will say.

When you are around a Red, you constantly get this vibe from them, "Hurry up, hurry up, hurry up. You're on the verge of wasting my valuable time." There's a certain amount of what the other colors would call, "arrogant entitlement" about Reds. Some Reds might agree and once again say, "What's problematic about that?"

54

To an independent Red who is a solo entrepreneur or a freelancer, this is no big deal. For a Red in the corporate or business world who wants professional advancement and higher remuneration, this can be problematic. Reds must learn how to listen with ears that hear, connect and be acknowledging to the people they work with and live with, if they are to ever gain respect and loyalty.

LITTLE QUIRK

A Red's little quirk is a result of that intense attitude they have. Sometimes Reds forget to bring other people along with their vision, and when they figure out that they've got a few people who don't like that, they get this attitude that goes something like this:

They stand up straight, put their shoulders back, chin down, give "the look" and then say something like...

TOUGH!
TOOO BAD, TOOOO SAD!
GET OVER IT!
GET TO THE POINT.
AND YOUR POINT IS?
NEXT!
DEAL WITH IT!
MOVE ON!
TALK TO THE HAND.

And of course the one that really moves the interaction along (sideways that is) ...

ARRIVEDERCI BABY & DON'T LET THE DOOR HIT YOU ON YOUR WAY OUT!

7

**Don't Worry, Be Happy
Yellows**

A Yellow showing up for work:

I'M HERE! HELLO EVERYBODY!
OK, YOU CAN ALL GET TO WORK NOW!
I'll come around and talk to you sometime soon. OK?
Hey, you! GET A SMILE ON THAT FACE!
DON'T WORRY, BE HAPPY.
IT'S GOING TO BE A GREAT DAY, DON'T YOU THINK!
SURE IT IS.

STRENGTHS

Yellows' mission in life is to make people happy. They see it as their gift, and it is the one and only thing that they do, in fact, take seriously. They believe life is meant to be lived and that everybody just needs to mellow out and be more like them: happy!

They are the great communicators and coordinators of people and events. Yellows are highly interactive and make great networkers. They are great in sales, because they are so charismatic. They are charismatic because they just like all people.

PAR-TAY!

Out of all of the colors, the Yellows are the least likely ever to be prejudiced about much of anything because that would certainly drag their happy energy down. If they are protective about anything it is their happiness and sunshiny dispositions.

As we saw earlier, Blues really do care about people. While Yellows appear to care, they really don't care in the same way as the Blues. They actually don't get that involved. They just enjoy people and basically see people as a form of entertainment! Yes, you are here for a Yellow to have a good time with, and that's more than enough in their opinion.

Yellows are busy, busy socializers and extremely effective networkers. They have a big job getting everybody happy, after all. This is their strength and they do it very well. Yellows bring people together in a fun way. They are generally the ones who organize get-togethers.

They love being around people and relish any job description that has the word "social" on it!

Yellows prefer to keep things "light" and when something is very serious or intense, it will be the Yellow who pops the funny one-liner that gets everybody off track and laughing.

Yellows generally can be great comedians as well. They have the innate ability to take something awful and make it funny.

Did I mention: They really do love making people happy.

Because Yellows are so charismatic, they can also step into leadership roles very easily.

The difference between a Yellow and a Red is that a Red leads from a place of an ordered plan and a Yellow will lead from a place of, "We'll create it as we go!" This generally drives the other three colors nuts, but hey, they all love the Yellow despite their unorthodox way of leading.

INTELLECT

A Yellow has a very creative mind and, unlike the Green, Yellows do not create within the confines of "the system." In fact, they are anything but systematic. Out of all the colors, the Yellow is outside the proverbial box more than they are in the box. They create in a place just a level beyond the Green's zone, known as the Great Out There!

Yes, the Great Out There is a fabulous place for the Yellows to mentally play and create. Because of this, they are more likely to be artists, musicians and any profession that requires the capacity to come up with new, Out There, never been done before, ideas.

I can always pick out the Yellows on the airplane when I travel, because they somehow schmoozed their way past all the signs that say, "Don't Board Yet," and they are already in their seats, strapped in, their eyes focused up beyond the ceiling of the plane in the Great Out There.

They have the biggest Gomer Pile Smile on their faces because they have already taken off! And trust me, they are having a good time. They don't really need people to keep themselves entertained. You can recognize Yellows a mile away by that constant big smile on their faces. Their smile is different from that of the Blues, in that it is as big as the state of Texas. They usually have big white teeth and when they smile, they make sure that every last tooth is shining through, just for you.

MOTTO

IF IT'S NOT FUN, I'M NOT DOING IT!

Now Greens need to pay close attention to this. If a Yellow is not going to do something, because it's not fun for them, who do you think will? That's right. A Green. Because a Green can't stand anything that's not getting done on time. And Yellows will dink around so long that a Green literally grabs it away from a Yellow and finishes the project.

It's like a Yellow can find a Green in the midst of the trees. Do you know what I'm saying here? A Yellow realizes that they don't think this particular project is fun, and so they start the search:

Here Greeny!
Here Greeny, Greeny!
Have I got a fun and elaborate P R O J E C T for you.
See how complicated it is?
See how you are the only one who can figure this out?
Oh Greeny, it is just for you.
Would you take it over from here?
Oh, you would!
Oh thank you.
Me?
Well, I'll just sit over here and learn from you, oh great Master!

All Greens need to take this pledge:

I PROMISE I WILL NOT GO NEAR A Yellow DURING THE WORK DAY!

I mean it Greens. I'm serious about this, because if you don't watch out, the Yellows will run away with you! There you are, doing their work and your work too. At the end of the day, the Greens are wiped out, collapsed on the ground. Their families are giving them blood transfusions for extra iron. And where are the Yellows!?

PAR-TAY!!!

Yellows clearly have the leadership qualities of a Tom Sawyer. Remember when Tom was supposed to be painting the fence white. One by one, he had convinced all the children in the neighborhood that he was having the most fun of anyone getting to paint that fence white and before long, they were all painting the fence and he was sitting there observing what a fine job they were doing!

PROBLEMATIC AREA

Most Yellows are probably thinking right now, "What problem? We don't have any problems!" Well maybe you don't, but other colors have some problems with you!

I understand that this may be a difficult concept for a Yellow, but it's true. There are some areas where it would certainly help make a few more people more happy, if you were to modify because ...

Yellows tend to get a little bit D I S T R A C T E D!

Yellows are the other color I mentioned earlier that thinks they can do ten things at once, but really can't. Here's what a typical work day can look like for a Yellow:

OK, let's answer all of the email first.
Oh, this looks like a fun project.
Oh, this also looks like a fun project too.
Hey, what about this fun thing I could be doing over here.
Hey Jessica!
Hi Sam!
Is it time for coffee yet?
Sure, I can hang out and visit...
Work?
Project?
What project?
Oh, that one.
Yes, I'll get it done.
When?
When it gets done.
Oh, I work better under pressure.
Sure, there's a mess on my desk, but I know where everything is.

Yellows prefer to work in what's known as a FREE-FORM WORK ENVIRONMENT.

What does that mean? A Yellow knows exactly what it means! It means, it gets done, when it gets done. OK? So, chill! Cool your jets. Get a smile on that face. Don't worry, be happy, eh?

Yellows will get things done, but it most likely will not be on a time line that any of the other colors prefer. That's not how they operate and that's not how they are wired.

Remember, they spend most of their time in the Great Out There. They are intellectually wired differently, and that's exactly why they are creative and solution generating.

'I work best under pressure.'

You will often hear a Yellow say that they do in fact believe that they work best under pressure. No one knows why this is. Just that it appears to work for this color. However, as a Yellow, it is important to understand that it hurts your credibility and your team participation, not to take this more seriously.

If you increase your credibility with people, it will make your life easier and happier when you are wanting to get the things across that you want.

As with all of the colors, you must have some give and take here, too. I realize that you think everybody else needs to get with your program to be happier; but that's not true if they are not wired for that intellectually, emotionally and psychologically.

To be a good team player you will want to work on your focus, stay tuned-in during meetings and being time conscious when it comes to projects. Why, you say? Because people are waiting on you and need you to do your part in a timely fashion. Okay? Turn it into something fun, and you won't be so resistant to what you perceive are the negative aspects to the more orderly personality styles.

For people who are working with Yellows: Yellows tell me that they don't mind being given "To Do Lists" or being checked in with repeatedly, as long as you don't use that condescending tone with them.

In other words, they accept that you need to control what they do, they accept that about you, and all they really want is for you to pull that attitudinal vibe of yours back in and keep it off of them and their work space. Got it?

LITTLE QUIRK

Yellows agree that their little quirk is that they:

JUST DON'T KNOW HOW TO DIAL IT DOWN

And many in our world would just like to wipe that smile right off their face. Yellows just don't get it that some people simply don't want to be happy, let alone all of the time. Yellows will say, "But we're so happy. We will undoubtedly live longer than anybody else."

To which other colors reply, "Of course, because you will be the extinction of anybody who has been over-infused with that big old, light-filled, smile of yours!"

I can't tell you how many 'good doer' Yellows I have run into in airports over the years. My focus is either on getting to my location or on making it home. When I've been schlepping my luggage through one too many airports, I am not at all in a mood to smile.

Invariably that's when a Yellow comes along, brightly and cheerfully gets right in my face and says,

"Hey there missy, get a smile on that face!"

I'm basically an unflappable person, but in those moments I just want to pick up my suitcase and... throw it at the wall!

Color Combos

"Synergy does not mean giving up what we want.
It means joining to co-create, so each is able to receive ever more
of what attracts us through joining rather than opposing."

-Barbara Marx Hubbard

As you were reading through the different Color Style descriptions did you find yourself thinking about someone else? Did you feel yourself gaining a new perspective? Were you thinking about your style and how it's either working for you or against you? Did you feel like you were more than one Color Style?

In presenting my *Connecting with Colors®* *Personality Styles* program to over 20,000 people in a two year period, I quickly discovered that the largest percentage of my audiences were experiencing havoc with their internal dialogue when it came to their Secondary Color Style. Most reported a noticeable incongruency when handling decision-making processes as well as their automatic reactions to intense situations.

Crazy-making Colors!

The inner dialogue between your Predominant Color Style and your Secondary Color Style can be crazy-making especially when you have not had this information to help you gain a broader perspective as to how your neurological wiring is impacting your communication, decisions and reactions. This may have not only been disconcerting for you, but also for the people you live, work and play with!

In addition to uncovering the importance of how the Secondary Color Styles can come into play, I then discovered that the Color Style people display at Work is not necessarily the same Color Style people go Home with! But it didn't stop there. Moving from one Color Style Hat to the next seemed to be happening in any one of the 7 Life Areas and so the million-dollar question became: "What can we do align all the different parts of ourselves so we can be taken seriously and command high regard from those we live, work and play with?"

While changing Color Style Hats seems to happen more with women than men, it can still happen with men as well.

Two Things to Consider

1. Our Secondary Color comes into play when making decisions and depending on the intensity of what Life is offering us, and...

2. Many people change Color Style Hats between Home and Work, Love, Sex and Money, Parenting and Teaching, 'Tweens and Teens, Leading and Management, and Sales.

Because of this "take it to the next level" feedback I was getting from my audiences, and to simplify this, I developed Personality Style Profiles—PSPs—in each of the **7 Life Areas of Interests** to help people understand more about what's going on internally.

Each Life Area PSP generates its own Individualized Report that shows what the scores are in each Color Style, and an explanation of how your Color Combo plays out in your reactions or decisions. And most importantly what you can be doing about conversations that are going side-ways.

In addition to understanding yourself in each Life Style Area, you are given a personalized explanation of exactly how you can easily "dial-in the other Color Styles" as conversations are unfolding. These recommendations are specific to your Color Style in both your Predominant and your Secondary Color Styles in relation to each of the other Color Styles.

Understanding just how pivotal this was and tremendously life transforming to my audiences, particularly with the women, has simplified my personality style system to make it completely understandable, easy to remember and immediately applicable for absolutely everyone!

'Wishy Washy' or a 'B...Barracuda?'

People who were being accused of being a Dr. Jekyll one minute and a Mr./Ms. Hyde the next, or being told they were "Wishy-Washy" a Jerk or B...barracuda one minute and a Placater the next or vice versa, have been so relieved—at long last—to finally understand what has been going on with their decision making processes and how they've been so ineffective in certain kinds of situations. The relief of this new understanding is palpable.

Based on the feedback you may have been receiving from the people who are making these not-so-lovely observations of you, it's perfectly normal to feel like there is something wrong with you which is never productive in being able to hold your own power in intense situations.

Then there is the residual effect of how much your inconsistency between your Colors can be diminishing your credibility with the very people you need to be connecting with in effective and synergistic ways.

So I brought in my *Attitudinal Energy: 30 Second Transformational Technique* (in Chapter 10) to help people ALIGN their Color Styles and DIAL-IN the Color Styles that they were not strong enough in, to help them navigate their way to credibility.

Your Color Combos

When you take any one of the 7 *Life Area Personality Style Profile*s tests, you will get an individualized report that shows you how you scored. Let's say, for example, your PSP Color Style scores are:

Red score: 8   Blue score: 3   Green score: 2   Yellow score: 7

What this is telling you is that your Color Combo's Primary Color is Red and your Secondary Color is Yellow, or you can say Red/Yellow.

There is not much going on in the Green (2) or Blue (3) areas with these scores. So think about what this means: this person (you!) has a director style who is focused on winning results, and is great at delegating (Red), so he or she can get out there and play, relax and have some fun as soon as possible (Yellow).

It's important to note that a Secondary Color can be very much at odds with the Primary Color. In the example I just mentioned, what can be confusing to others about the Red/Yellow is that one minute the Red/Yellow may be off-putting to others, speaking harshly, while directing in-your-face commands about what should be done right here, right now, because Red/Yellow is totally focused on getting those RESULTS yesterday (Red). However, in the next moment, Yellow takes over, is really FUN, charismatic and engaging, making everyone around them feel as though there's all the time in the world.

Remember: The more intense the situation, the more the Primary Color will dominate.

In the Red/Yellow example we just discussed, a person with this score will, under pressure, become more intense about time schedules and the need to get things done. On the other hand, if the Color Combo was the opposite, with Yellow as Primary and Red as Secondary (a Yellow/Red), the more intense the situation, the more Yellow that person is likely to become and will try to "lighten things up" by popping off funny one-liners and exhibiting delightful off-the-cuff wit.

The GOAL *here is to* ALIGN *your colors,*

by DIALING-IN *between the two.*

As you may have realized with these Color Combo examples, there are as many variations of Color Combos as there are people. Regardless, no matter what Color Combo your PSP Scores give you, the GOAL here is to ALIGN your colors, and you do this by DIALING-IN between the two Color Styles.

You will do this with my #1 favorite Behavior Modification technique I like to call: Let's Make A Deal!

Let's Make A Deal!

If your Color Combo is problematic for you then it is time for you to integrate these two colors and start thinking "rainbow effect." You will sit down with a notepad and listen to both Color Styles versions of how they'd prefer to proceed. Somewhere in the middle of the two ways of approaching the decision or the task at hand will come a way to do it that both Color Styles within you can agree to i.e., Let's Make A Deal!

This is paramount to coming across to others as a credible, competent and capable person and it is the very thing that will energetically send a message that you are a person of stature, focus and to be highly regarded.

What People Are Saying: Different Color Hats!

"I wish I had taken Mary's Life Area PSPs years ago."

Michelle Fought discovered that her at-home dominant color was very different from her color on the job.

"At the start of my Connecting with Colors Synergize Your Life Program that I took from Mary, I took both the Home and the Work Personality Style Profile—PSPs. Although from the training I had a good idea of my Style, I was curious what my Secondary Color Styles were. I was shocked to find out that, while I knew I was a Yellow—in fact a very bright and shiny Yellow—in the work world, at Home I was a Predominant Red!

"What?! I'm a Red Mom?!" Taking that PSP (Personality Style Profile) opened my eyes as to how I was communicating at home.

It made so much sense! After all these years of raising children, I finally "got it" why my own kids didn't think I was as much fun as everybody else on the planet. And the bullhorn I used at school in a fun, and entertaining way wasn't so much fun when I used it to get their butts out of bed in the morning—go figure! The awareness from taking that PSP began my process of "dialing -in" to their colors. It has really improved the communication in our home! And I can still have fun with my bullhorn!"

Michelle Fought,
CWC Synergize Your Life Participant
ConnectingWithColors/SYL

"Mary's PSPs have really helped me to not feel left out emotionally."

Maureen Ross Gemme found new insight in her relationship with her husband by understanding their Color Style differences.

"I've been studying different personality type indicators for years and most are pretty complex. Mary's program breaks it down to simple, yet quite accurate, color styles.

I'm kind of a raging Yellow and I discovered that my husband is totally Green. In learning about Greens, I discovered WHY he always wants to do projects by himself. It's not because he doesn't want to include me, it's just that he truly believes he has a better way, doesn't delegate well and doesn't need my far-out ideas! And then when I voice my idea anyway, and he feels criticized, I remember that he's neurologically wired this way and now I can easily explain that to him and in fact hold back when his way is working just fine. He apparently criticizes himself enough for the both of us!

73

This knowledge has really helped me to not feel left out emotionally. Mary's Personality Style Profile (PSP) has helped me with my Blue friends and my Red boss too. I intend to make a living out of sharing Mary's Color Styles with others to spread the knowledge and create more peace in the world!"

Maureen Ross Gemme,
CWC Synergize Your Life Participant
ConnectingWithColors.com/SYL

Remember this: Personality Styles is not an exact science. It IS however, in the way I have incorporated it into each of the PSPs Life Style Areas, easy to understand, remember, apply, enjoy and have FUN with to make the world a much better place to live.

This is the time to heal generational legacies of pain, once and for all. What Life Areas are most problematic for you right now? Home? Work? Love, Sex and Money? Parenting and Teaching? 'Tween and Teens? Leading and Management? Sales?

Go take the quick PSP test! Once you see how simple this is you will feel instant relief because knowing how you are showing up for the various demands life is offering you can give you an amazing new perspective. Instead of nagging, complaining, arguing, fussing and being continuously upset about how things are going, sit down with the people within your circle of influence and begin a new, productive and synergizing conversation once you've all taken the various PSPs. The PSPs truly are transformational and life changing and certainly worth your time and investment.

To take your own Individualized PSP—Personality Style Profile—in any one or all of the 7 Life Areas go to:

ConnectingWithColors.com/PSP

Part III Aligning Relationships

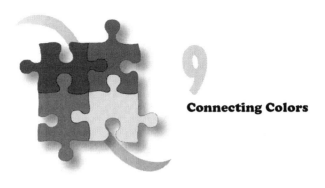

Connecting Colors

I think you go around with the insane delusion
that people like you!

–Woody Allen, Deconstructing Harry

Research indicates that in 80% of the cases where people are pink-slipped, downsized, or just plain fired, it's not due to a lack of technological know-how or competence. It's because they are not able to deal with personal differences and emotional situations within the work environment.

Now, more than ever before, we need to figure out how to "get along." The demands on our attention, energy and time are greater than ever before because of this techno age that we live in.

Productivity expectations increase as the technology speeds up our ability to get things out and make things happen. Instead of a project taking ten weeks to design, that same project may now be expected to be completed in ten days!

There is nothing wrong with any of this, but it does demand that people communicate with each other in ways that accomplish a mutual understanding, and that they find a way to commit and go forward, whether or not they agree in this given moment in time.

One common theme I see, as I work with teams in the corporate environment, is this belief that we all have to agree before there can be forward movement! One company, where I led extensive training seminars, has a motto that they use: Disagree and then Commit!

When I've asked if this works for them, the consensus is that it works… and it can still be challenging at first. We are human after all, and we all tend to be a bit stubborn about holding on to the notion that my way is the only way. So what do we do about this?

Demystify compatibility! Compatibility, or the lack of it, is not such a mystery. Both rapport and tension are rather predictable, once you know what to look for.

What Motivates People?

Communication breakdown comes from failing to understand other people. We don't listen to other people, and we try to talk a language that we expect people to understand, when in fact they are listening and speaking in another language, "their" language.

With so many ways to interpret other people's behavior, why not take time to remove some of the guesswork.

The Colors Connection

Your behavior is affected by the situations you're in. Your social style is the result of many years of development. No personality style is better than any other, yet you enhance your relationship with others if you understand your motivations, strengths and problematic areas, and those of people around you.

Whether I'm working with families in bringing more harmony to their personal relationships or whether I am brought in to corporations to work on aligning Communication, Leadership and/or Team Synergism, the first thing we do is determine the Predominant Communication Styles of all participants.

Understand that we all have a little bit of every color. What we are most interested in is where you dig your heels in during difficult encounters — which is your Predominant Color.

This is where confusion, conflict and heated interactions begin. What we want to do is to not only learn about ourselves, but also start thinking about the style that is most difficult to deal with and communicate to. By understanding what we personally value, how we think and integrate information, and how others are similar or differ, we can easily see the effect these things have on our interactions.

For starters, people with similar tendencies are most compatible with one another socially. That's because those with common interests, habits and approaches help reinforce each other's self-esteem.

In the work arena when it comes to tasks—whether it's doing a project at work, purchasing materials or determining the budget —the dynamics differ dramatically.

For example, Reds and Yellows share an outward focus and often similar competitive interests. Blues and Greens, on the other hand are both inwardly oriented and may like the same kinds of activities. Both Yellows and Blues aspire to be in relationships, yet they each enjoy their social interactions differently. It's the Blue who's in the giving, caretaking role and trying to make peace, while the Yellow is trying to get everybody to "lighten-up" and just have some fun!

Meanwhile, the "I want it and I want it now" directive Reds and the networking Yellows commonly find it hard to develop rapport with the quiet, focused and internally driven Blues and Greens, who are less decisive and driven toward external rewards. Blues and Greens, in turn, find the Reds less desirable because they're too pushy, too loud and often too bossy in their demands of them and how they communicate with other people.

To the Red, who just wants results and wants them yesterday, and to the Yellow, whose basic saying is, "Don't worry, be happy!"—the cautious Green and steady Blue can be a drag. While Blues often resign themselves to tolerate the "put it all out there" forwardness of Reds and Yellows, the Green frequently prefers to be left alone in his or her work space.

So what happens, now that you know your type and you work with a type that polarizes you? In the next chapter, you will discover that the *30-second-or-less* solution you seek lies in how you decide to connect, attitudinally.

*Treat a person as he is,
and he will remain as he is.
Treat a person as if he were
what he could be,
and he will become
what he could and should be.*

– Goethe

Matching & Mirroring

The technique for aligning any and all combinations of Color Styles that we are going to work with is called *Matching & Mirroring*.

Richard Bandler and John Grinder first developed this technique through their Neuro-Linguistic Program or NLP. Neuro-Linguistic Programming is an approach to organizational change based on "a model of interpersonal communication chiefly concerned with the relationship between successful patterns of behavior and the subjective experiences (especially patterns of thought) underlying them" and "a system of alternative therapy based on this, which seeks to educate people in self-awareness and effective communication, and to change their patterns of mental and emotional behavior."

The co-founders, Richard Bandler and linguist John Grinder, claimed it would be instrumental in "finding ways to help people have better, fuller and richer lives." They coined the title to denote their belief in a connection between neurological processes ("neuro"), language ("linguistic") and behavioral patterns that have been learned through experience ("programming") and that can be organized to achieve specific goals in life.

Not only were Bandler and Grinder on to something decades ago, even the newest research supports that imitation is good in relationships because it can make you seem more appealing.

In experiments at Radboud University of Nijmegen in the Netherlands, subjects interviewed by someone who subtly mirrored their postures gave bigger donations to a charity and were more likely to help an interviewer. And in research published in the Journal of Personality and Social Psychology, students rated interactions with mimickers as smoother than those with non-mimickers; they also considered mimickers more likable.

According to Robert Epstein, Ph.D., lecturer and former editor of Psychology Today. "But while imitation may seem simple, it can be tricky. If people notice what you're doing, they may find you manipulative."

Each communication style is based on what a person values and how he or she thinks psychologically and neurologically.

The intent of *Matching & Mirroring* is to understand that principle. You'll physically Match and Mirror those persons you are interacting with, which in turn helps you start dialing-in their personality style: how they think, how they like to learn, how they talk, what they like and dislike.

Think smaller: If someone crosses his or her legs, wait five to ten seconds, then cross your ankles. If subtlety's not your strong suit, make note of a person's mannerisms. Then try a few mini-versions the next time you're together.

It has nothing to do with greater-than or less-than comparisons. It's about the diversity of individual "wiring" for thinking, learning, understanding, and the values this diversity creates within every one of us.

3 Steps to
Matching & Mirroring

1: Get in Sync!

Match the person's body language, voice tone, attitude and verbal language. If they are standing or sitting with their shoulders back and quite erect, do the same thing.

If they use language succinctly, be succinct. Don't go on about your personal or their personal life. Match their interests. If they are interested in Results, keep your conversation with them quick and to the point. This, by the way, would be a Red.

Be Nice with a Blue, soften your stance, your shoulders and your voice. Allow a connection to take place first by asking them about their day or how their family is. When discussing an area of concern, simply give them illustrative and/or descriptive information with an example of how you'd prefer it to be. They are driven by knowledge, and their key desire is to figure it out so they can do it well and be of service to you. Appreciate that!

Think Systems with a Green; talk systems and talk fast! They already see the "big picture" so what they are interested in is the mental process of designing the most efficient way to get there.

What about the fun-loving, people-oriented **Yellows**? Simply **Open Up** and put a big old smile on your face, then pull up a chair and sit down. Why? Because it's going to be a while. They will want to connect with you for at least 15 to 20 minutes before getting down to business. Once down to business though, watch out, because they are about to razzle dazzle you with their most creative and innovative ideas to help make that event you are coordinating a spectacular success!

2: Get in The Driver's Seat

Take responsibility for the conversation. Don't expect them to read your mind and magically give you what you want. Stop giving yourself the luxury or excuses about "what's wrong with them" and get laser-focused on building rapport with the people you work, live and play with. You will accomplish that by honoring how they integrate information based on their style. Do not expect them to match your style; get your rear in gear and match theirs.

Blues will often ask, "Will the Reds start being nice to the Blues when the Blues start matching and mirroring them?"

I understand that you've been wishing all along that Reds would be nice like you, but that's not the goal here. The intention is to be effective and unifying in your communication with Reds or any color for that matter. You can't afford to be resentful about being the one who is making the change.

Rather than denying negative emotions, view them as choices. You can choose to be angry in response to frustrating circumstances.

Or you can choose to keep your cool, assess the situations objectively and decide on a course of action to solve the problem. That is, utilizing the *Matching & Mirroring* technique will align you with others instead of separating you from them further.

3: Get an Attitude Adjustment!

You can't have an attitude and keep it a secret! Give Up the need to label anything as right or wrong, good or bad and you begin the transformational process within seconds. As I said earlier, we all tend to believe that our way is the best way or the only way, right?

This attitudinal energy is inflammatory, and it causes more alienation in productivity than any other denominator. Judgment, condemnation and entitlement all cause rifts, resentments and undercurrents, which are completely destructive to the culture of an organization.

Make a habit of looking for the best in other people, and be generous with sincere praise, regard and compliments.

Possibly the most important work we will ever do in this life is the work we do in relationships. There is nothing more important, because when we leave this world, it will be the quality of the life we lived and how we made people feel when they were with us that will be everlasting.

Remember this: you can't fail at this, you can only get results. If you don't like the results you are getting, then it's time to try something new! The real Power behind identifying the colors is learning to take the risk of aligning yourself with people who are not of your like mind.

The intent of this effort is to soften the hard mental constructs that we often use to deal with each other and our differences.

To go deeper with this information, and to learn more about how you can transform all of your relationships—even the most impossible ones—into harmonious experiences, check out:

Connecting with Colors®
SYNERGIZE Your Life Program

This transformational program explores in-depth techniques for understanding exactly how each of the 4 Color Style operate in the 7 Areas of Life most important to us: Work, Home, Love/Sex/Money, Parenting/Teaching, Tweens/Teens, Leadership/Management and Sales. To learn more, go to:

ConnectingWithColors.com/Program

The Power of One

I am only one,
but still I am one.
I cannot do everything,
but still I can do something;
and because I cannot do everything
I will not refuse to do something I can do.

-Edward Everett Hale

Our color personality is evident in everything we do in life, not only in business settings, or interpersonal relationships, but even in how we tackle routine chores.

Washing Your Car!

One of the best ways to identify your personality as well as your Predominant Color is how you wash your car. Here is how network marketer Lane Winsett describes the different personalities in terms of washing your car:

GREEN

A Green goes into the kitchen to get his car keys on a key rack. Next he walks out to the garage and presses the automatic garage door opener. He backs the car out to the driveway where he always washes the car. Next he goes to the cabinet where he gets his pail, sponge and magic soap. Then he goes to the hose roller and unrolls the hose, pours in just the right amount of soap in the pail for the right consistency, then he methodically begins to wash the car from the top down.

You know a Green would never wash a car from the bottom up! And then of course after he has it nice and soapy, he starts to rinse it from the top down to get it exactly the way he wants it. After that he uses his chamois, because all Greens have a chamois!

After he has it nice and dry, he'll put all the rubber tire dressings on, the interior dressings, clean the windows with newspaper because Greens know that it doesn't leave streaks. Once he's got the car meticulously clean he then puts everything back, pulls the car back into the garage, presses the automatic garage door, takes the keys and puts them back up on the rack exactly where they belong in the kitchen.

RED

How does a Red wash the car? He drags the hose out and suds up the car, rinses the car off, hops in the car starts driving down the expressway for his next appointment to dry it off. He leaves everything exactly where it is because he's got things to do, places to go, people to boss so there's really no time to put things away. Besides, someone else can pick up after him!

YELLOW

True to Your Color!

How does a Yellow wash the car? The car wash, dummy! There's no one to talk to in the Yellow's own garage, or in the driveway, and he doesn't want to get his fingernails dirty. Remember he is a social creature and he likes to be out there in an environment where he can meet people to talk and socialize. What better place than sitting at the snack bar at the car wash, visiting with everybody that walks by, while other people vacuum it, wash it, shine it and deodorize it!

BLUE

How do Blues wash a car... they don't! They are not out to impress anybody! They have peace signs, and dents and dings, and bumper stickers that say, 'Save the Whales.'

What does this all mean for you now?

The bottom line is that once you start to observe people's behavior, you will be able to identify the personality characteristic traits that they might possess, what colors they might be, what language they might speak. And once you begin to speak people's language and listen in their language, they'll be able to identify with you as you identify with them.

What does this do? It increases productivity and allows for you to be a happier, healthier person at work, at home. Once you become a master communicator, you'll find a tremendous amount of happiness in your life. You can draw from your own reservoir of power, knowing this:

You possess all four colors in your personality!

The next time you have a project you need to get done, and you are feeling distracted and are procrastinating, say to yourself, "I really need to dial-in Red about this." Get action-oriented, get it done now. You'll be amazed at what you can get done when you "get Red" about something.

Let's say you are a Red and you have a management meeting to attend where there will be a lot of input from a lot of people. You tell yourself, I need to dial-in a little more Yellow going into this meeting to get more creative and to stimulate greater solution-generating ideas.

Or you may decide that you need to dial-in a little more Blue to be more of a team player. Maybe you've decided you need to be a better listener, more compassionate in regard to people's thoughts and feelings and the dynamics that are happening between team members.

You may decide you need to dial-in a little more Green and be more system oriented so you can design an effective, orderly solution.

Borrow The Strengths of Other Colors

You will be amazed at what happens when you go into that meeting intentionally utilizing the strengths of the other three styles. You will come out of that meeting knowing that because you elected to be "mindful," you not only participated synergistically with that team, you helped them accomplish their goals quickly and creatively!

You know the other times you've seen things happen in companies where they run up against a wall or they have a specific problem that they have not been able to resolve. That's the time to kick your shoes off, put your feet up on the desk, get out a piece of paper and pencil and dial-in Yellow. Start to think about an innovative idea to overcome that mountain. When the idea comes in, take it to a **Green**; he or she will collaborate with you on designing a system to make it happen.

You'll be amazed at what will happen when you allow your "creative" mind to really start to take hold. But, if that's not an easy adaptation for you to dial into, just go to a **Yellow** person in the company and say, "Hey, what creative ideas do you have for solving this?" See the Yellow's eyes light up with anticipation of going to the Great Out There to find a creative solution. Take what he gives you to a Green to formulate the system to bring the Yellow's idea from the Great Out There down to earth so it can be implemented.

BLUES, being knowledge seekers, are the first ones to hit the Internet to search for the "whys" and "hows," which then moves them into effective implementation of whatever new idea the Yellows came up with that the Greens designed a system for, so the Blues can implement it while the **REDS** are taking the lead to delegate and to find even more problems to solve!

I was watching a Home & Garden TV show about the new wave of home rehab and do-it-yourselfers, and the host interviewed a husband and wife about how they went about building their new deck onto the back of their house.

The husband was interviewed first and he said that he had really, really wanted to get this deck done for quite awhile but couldn't figure out how to go about it or where to start. He had procrastinated for several years and finally his wife searched the Internet.

The wife, being a Blue, was a knowledge seeker and once she understood her husband's real reason for procrastinating (he didn't know where to start), she browsed the Internet and found a new website for the do-it-yourselfer, and searched for a plan that would fit the back of their house. She printed out the directions, which gave specifics on where to start. It gave detailed information on what kind and quantity of wood and other materials to purchase. So she studied it, made some innovative revisions to meet the needs of their house, completed the drawings, then handed it to her husband for him to buy the materials and start building.

Her husband said he was more than ready to get going with the project once he knew where to start. Now, he had a plan. His wife, a Blue, had brought him a (visual) plan with innovative revisions, directions and specifications with end results. He was clearly a Red and like most Reds he is now in his own turf and he will direct the show from here.

You can tell that he wasn't a Yellow, because a Yellow would have started the project by simply waiting for the first sunny day, going out and buying a bunch of lumber and several sacks of screws, nuts and bolts. He would have invited several friends over, purchased a few cases of beer, called in a pizza order and then, thrown the thing together as it happened.

91

You know neither of them were Greens because Greens would definitely have been able to see the deck in their mind from beginning to end. They'd have drawn it out, and created a system for undertaking the project without the help of the Internet. Then, just for the mental fun of it, Greens would have gone to the Internet just to firm up what they thought needed to happen in the first place, and to establish and confirm a most conservative estimate of materials. The Greens would have gone out and purchased the exact materials needed and started it all by themselves.

You see how you can use not only your own gifts and talents, but also borrow from other people's skills. Each and every one of these colors allows you to build on to your own personality style. Just because it's your preferred color, it doesn't mean you are limited to only one way of approaching things or people.

How The First Freeway Was Built!

Yellow comes up with the idea, "Hey wouldn't it be great to drive from NYC to LA on one freeway, one stretch of road?"

The Blue person said "Who's going to negotiate with all those farm guys when we cut through all of those pastures?"

The Green guy said, "Well hey, it's a great idea and we better put some signs and limits and restrictions on the freeway or somebody's going to get killed. Greens are thinking about the system that needs to be put in place for safety, structure, rules and regulations.

What did the Red guy say? He said, "Now that we have a starting point, I know who can build it, and I'll orchestrate it and delegate it so it can get built. I'll make sure it gets done."

Each of one of those personalities works together to accomplish a common goal. And that's what your place of work, or your family can do once you learn how to pull all those talents and abilities together synergistically.

To Make a Big Difference, learn to recognize what colors are dominant in others and how to use this knowledge for better communication and understanding of other people.

Make A Big Difference!

How people want to be communicated to:

Red people are direct and want a straightforward approach with focus on short-term goals and immediate results.

Yellow people are accommodating, flexible; they want to be consulted as to their opinions, and they want to feel that they are an integral part of the group.

Blue people are knowledge-based, and they ask questions in order to have time to assess alternatives and problems. They don't like to be pressured into rapid action.

Green people are more reserved and cautious, they need verification and justification, and they want documentation before any decision is made. They are certainly not individuals to be rushed.

You can now see that each and every one of these personality styles is different, and we need to respect each other's color traits. You have everything you need to be a powerful communicator and a marvelous living example of what humanity can be!

Becoming a TurnAround Specialist

Now, more than ever before, we need to figure out how to connect harmoniously. A knowledge of Color Styles and a conscious application of the theory help us survive this techno-age in which we live, where the demands on our attention, energy and time are greater than ever before.

The technological revolution in the last three decades has dramatically changed every aspect of our lives, at home and school as well as in traditional work environments, and a Worldwide economic downturn is forcing downsizing and greater demands for work productivity.

There is nothing wrong with these expedited goals, but our accelerated schedule does require communication between individuals in ways that promote understanding. Whether or not they find a way to agree in this given moment of time, our high-speed society demands that they determine how to commit and go forward.

Your Own Color Style Experiment

For the next two weeks, each time you feel resistant or have a fear thought about others and their behavior, ask yourself:

"If I were going to be a TurnAround Specialist in this situation, what could I do?"

- **What Color Style are they speaking in right now?**

Blue: efficient, selfless, helpers, huggers and caring about relationships.

Green: systems, projects, thinking, going fast and not delegating easily.

Red: competitive, leader, winners and not necessarily listening.

Yellow: social, happy, talkative and deflecting negativity with wit.

- **Match & Mirror their language, body physiology and posture, vibe and tone.**

- **Look for new evidence about a bigger picture.** What's trying to happen here? What's the opportunity in this? Shift your perception of the situation as quickly as possible.

- **Practice dialing down your fear, suspend judgment and shift your attitude.** At the very least, pull your attitudinal energy back in, and think: before I can change anybody else, what can I change about myself?

- **Get in touch with your attitude that a certain person really is the biggest jerk on the planet.** Remember that you can change your attitude in increments. Don't worry; this is just an experiment; so you cannot fail, you can only get results. If you don't like your results then change them by talking about what you prefer.

- **Give up your right to keep a hold over this person in your mind.** You are the one losing here. Anger towards another doesn't hurt that person at all, but it's negatively affecting your physiology. Do this, and I guarantee you will see a softening in your communication exchanges with those you are interacting with. It's really up to you to determine how this will play out.

• **Listen intuitively and be mindful of inferiority projections of negative labels from the past.** They just may not be thinking what you think they are thinking. Remember, the resistance can be as simple as a Color Style issue.

• **Be accommodating with each other's idiosyncrasies, when people are just emotionally "in their stuff."** It's like blowing up a balloon. Release the stem before tying, and all the air comes rushing out instantly.

What Are YOU Projecting?

A great rule of thumb, before you accuse someone of having a bad attitude about you, is to investigate first. Don't assume that your first evaluation of the situation is absolutely true. Double-check by asking people what might be going on for them that causes the behavior you're confused about.

Ask several questions with an interest in their answers, no matter what their answer will be. This is what emotionally maturing and healthy individuals do to effectively lead peaceful and harmonious lives.

Investigate & Doublecheck!

Being the leader of your own life is never about running away and it's never about rushing forward. It's about slowing down, taking a breath and starting to apply what you are learning.

Time Outs are an excellent cooling-down mechanism unless you are using them to try to control what someone else is doing or not doing:

- to "teach them a lesson" by triggering their fear of abandonment (Blue),

- to make them wait on you for hours (Green),

- to try to be the winner with the last say (Red), or

- to blow them off completely (Yellow).

'I think in the end, when you're famous...

people like to narrow you down to a few personality traits. I think I've just become this ambitious, say-whatever's-on-her-mind, intimidating person. And that's part of my personality, but it's certainly not anywhere near the whole thing.'

- Madonna Ciccone

Guess what her Predominant Color Style is?

As we seek to understand others through our different Color Styles, a natural path opens up and can bring about alignment—even between polar opposites. When we attempt to understand an alternative viewpoint, there is a shift in our thought process and we are more willing to listen and perceive what someone else is trying to communicate.

This kind of connection is about more than simple acknowledgment; it's about the necessity of reaching out daily to be emotionally available, through compassionate understanding, to the individuals in our lives, regardless of who they are or what they've done.

You can make a difference in how well individuals are able to function, both at home and out in the world, by the kind of understanding— followed by skill development—you decide to give them.

Suspicion, skepticism, anger, disappointment, minimizing or abandoning never produce positive, productive results. And, in fact, avoidance kills credibility and effectiveness just as fast as overpowering, berating and using other fear or force tactics.

The next time you hear yourself say, "But this person is impossible to deal with," simply stop and take thirty seconds to consider what it's like to live in their shoes and more importantly, what it's like trying to communicate with you!

The 3-Step Dance

Think of this information as a way to practice a 3-Step Dance. 1-2-3, 1-2-3, 1-2-3.

In the face of any situation, you now have all the tools you need to practice asking yourself just three questions:

1. What's their Color Style right now?

2. How can I Match & Mirror them to get in sync with them?

3. What's my real attitude about this person?

When you remain consistent in offering an understanding connection in a positive and behavior-affirming way, it becomes a "conscious" act that offers profound healing to a situation.

It is from a place of understanding that you can effectively move forward into skill development that is needed to regulate and ultimately dissolve a problematic situation.

This, coupled with a decision simply to slow down and energetically connect with individuals, will create alignment that generates the long-term solutions you seek.

Oh, and take a breath and lighten up a little bit so you can have some fun with this!

And while the 4 Color Styles information is transformative in and of itself, we're really not done yet.

Keep Learning and Keep Going Forward

You've learned some extremely important information in this book and the key to working things out effectively in every area of our lives is dependent on you applying what you have just learned to life's situations.

Our tendency is to continue to step back into doing the thing that is not working — like avoidance, fighting the same old fight, pushing back or collapsing into powerlessness — thinking that if we only believe more, try harder, hang in there just a little bit longer, the unhappy situation will eventually change.

The goal here is to keep stepping forward in learning effective and strategic methods of relating—getting ourselves back into school so to speak - by taking additional Color Style course work in the 7 Areas of Life that are most important to our entire existence: Work, Home, Love/Sex/Money, Parenting/Teaching, Tweens/Teens, Leading/Managing and Sales.

Now is the time to keep expanding your understanding—to gently and progressively learn what more you need to know in order to deal confidently and effectively with the difficult situations and people in your life and not wait for things to build to the point of eruption or devastation.

The Cruel Frog Experiment

Several experiments involving recording the reaction of frogs to slowly heated water took place in the 19th century, which even though cruel, illustrate exactly how the psyche remains committed to the insanity of "doing the same thing over and over again expecting different results" even though it may be completely miserable or uncomfortable. This experiment simply signifies what can happen when we live an unexamined life:

Phase 1 of the experiment: The scientists dropped a frog into scalding water. The frog jumped out immediately, and saved its own life by doing so. You and I would do the same. If we find ourselves in extreme pain or imminent danger, we flee immediately.

Phase 2 of the experiment: Was to put the frog in a pan with tepid water and place the pan on a burner. The fire under the pan was turned up ever so slowly, until ultimately it was boiling. The frog did not jump out and ultimately died.

This cruel experiment illustrates that in not doing anything new or productive about difficult people or challenging life situations we literally set ourselves up for undesirable experiences.

There is of course a **Catch-22** in all of this. Even though what's going on is completely undesirable we fear that if we speak up it's going to possibly get more undesirable … Right?

What this illustrates about our current paradigm is that—lacking a shocking, disruptive event—we tolerate a slow and steady increase of pain. It is numbing, rather than alarming. We have been taught to be accepting of this idea that we are basically powerless to change the situations and approaches in our lives that are harmful.

Our co-workers and family members generally do not encourage us to take our innate power and initiative to interrupt, alter or change it. Why? Because it may bump up against their fear of not rockin' the boat, keep things status quo, and the belief that there is something wrong with doing something that "might" make somebody else unhappy about being confronted with things that simply are not okay.

This of course, is based on the assumption—belief—that to change one's experience with difficult people and situations requires a period when things must get worse before getting better. That it's going to be confrontational, messy, loud, angry, scary, unpredictable and awful.

But think about it. Isn't the situation difficult right now? This is a perfect example of:

Frog Think!

Understand that learning "effective" and strategic ways to think, speak and listen are "skills" that simply must be learned and then applied one simple step at a time getting more and more confidence and successful outcomes, as you learn and grow.

It's the little things that,

when repeated over time,

will yield either huge success
or debilitating failure and loss.

It's the little things that build the neurological structure of our minds and determine repeat performances of those things that are working, as well as all those things that aren't working. We find that it gradually becomes somewhat comfortable to feel uncomfortable and unhappy in our lives, because it is the known, the guaranteed.

To change it would be a risk. That's why people have more heart attacks on Mondays than any other time. It's about having to go back to that job, where the heat has been turned up gradually over time until it literally kills them to remain there. The "heat" can be a variety things: a inharmonious work place, or the loss of passion and purpose in that particular form of work and the belief that one has no power to change life's circumstances.

Here are some Frog Speak reasons we tell ourselves to let well enough alone:

I am powerless to change things.

I have no control anyway, why bother?

This is just too hard.

There will be backlash – hell to pay!

They will turn it around on me and tell me I'm the crazy one.

It takes too much time and energy to bother with them. They are impossible.

What's the use, they will never change.

I hate upsetting anyone when asking them to change.

And the most debilitating of them all, in Frog Speak is, "It's not really that bad."

Certainly there are many situations in life that just aren't that bad, however, if you hear yourself saying this repeatedly, then start paying attention to what's coming out of your mouth! It's a clue.

Here are some **Frog Reactions** in how we've handled difficult people and situations in the past that are not working.

We have been known to:

Get angry

Get in people's faces

Emotionally check out

Leave

Threaten

Minimize or bypass it all together

Use blame, shame, guilt and disappointment to get them to
  GET IT

Become invisible

Catch-22

So in that way we are like the frog but the undercurrents are always there with the potential to heat up and affect our healthy, energy and state of mind because we're not doing anything to remedy the situation because we don't have the knowledge.

Let's Get Honest!

As you were reading this book were you thinking about somebody else while I was going through the Color Style descriptions?

Were you were thinking about Your style and how it's either working for you or not working for you?

Here's the thing:

NOTHING IMPROVES UNTIL WE IMPROVE IT!

It's the little things that, when repeated over time, will yield either huge success or debilitating failure and loss.

The amazing thing that's most likely been happening while you've been reading this book is that people are literally changing before your very eyes because you are seeing them differently.

At the beginning this book I told you about how I open my speaking engagements by asking my audiences, "How many of you live or work with difficult people?"

Now I'm going to ask you:

"Do you just WISH the difficult people in your life would change so you don't have to?"

I hope this information has got you motivated to Take Your Life and Your Power back. I hope you are so entirely motivated by the Color Styles information that you will run out to your family and friends and inspire them to take the Personality Style Profile test in every applicable area of life so that you can discover what's really been going on in all of your relationships.

We can talk about what people are and aren't doing all day long every single day and nothing will change.

The only person with the power is **YOU.** The power to learn more, to go deeper and gain even more understanding and then take it to the people you care about so you can apply it together.

I want to see you taking this **ALL THE WAY** ... to the best relationship experiences imaginable.

While the 4 Color Styles information in this book is transformative in and of itself, there is more that you can learn and do to

POSITIVELY TURNAROUND

those people and those situations that life offers us, and make a lasting difference.

I find that once people understand where the communication breakdown is occurring and that it is transformational in and of itself. The solutions we seek come from **SEEING** with **EYES** of understanding first, and that softening helps us communicate more intuitively.

And if you are ready to go deeper with this, I've got a companion program for you on page 116 where you can learn exactly what's happening in each of the 7 Life Areas, with immediately applicable techniques that will dissolve conflict in most cases in 30 seconds or less.

The beauty of this kind of information is really what you choose to do with it from this point forward. Labeling people attitudinally is not going to be productive. But thinking in these terms is going to help you relate and understand.

There is nothing so sweet as **SYNERGY** between two or more people and there is nothing more de-energizing as negative undercurrents of resentment, judgment, disappointment, skepticism, misunderstanding and people checking out mentally, emotionally and physically from the relationship or showing up belligerent, argumentative, oppositional, defiant or minimizing the importance of the situation.

AND there's even more that you can learn to do about those kind of intense situations.

According to Dr. Deepak Chopra...

KNOWLEDGE HAS REORGANIZING POWER IN IT

❝ Using effort to consciously practice an attitude or to cultivate a mood is unnecessary and can cause stress and strain. Relevant knowledge has organizing power inherent in it. It is simply enough to know, to be aware of the principles; taking in new positive knowledge will be processed and metabolized by our bodies, and the results will be spontaneous. The results do not occur overnight, but begin to manifest gradually over a period of time.

As we take in new, relevant knowledge every day, it is more likely that our attitude and behavior will change spontaneously, without any effort on our part.

Read relevant—positive—information once a day, listen to positive, educational audio's once a day, then you will see the changes that happen spontaneously in your life and the effortless ease with which wealth and affluence come into your life. ")

This is how you create new neurological pathways to SEE and understand more about what's going on from a higher perspective. And in doing so:

CONNECTION TURNs 'ME' INTO 'WE,' WHICH = SYNERGY

In the very last section of this book I have provided you with the information of several of my transformative NEXT STEP Programs that you can study at home or practice at work. Advance your career and make a positive change by training those you work with to SYNERGIZE, by understanding the 4 Color Styles and how they come into play in every conversation.

For starters, the companion program to this book, **Connecting with Colors® SYNERGIZE Your Life with The 4 Personality Styles Program** will shift you—and the people you care about—quickly out of any relational suffering!

How many of you have sat and listened to a good friend or colleague's problems, and no amount of advice has helped?

To show you just how quickly a transformation can occur with someone for whom nothing has previously worked, I will share a story about one of my coaching clients.

In one session near Mother's Day, my client was experiencing emotional suffering, because her 27-year-old daughter had cut off all communication with her. Her daughter was upset about her mother's fearful worry and excessive interfering in her life, even though there were significant and legitimate areas of concern in the daughter's life.

These concerns were magnified by my client's (Blue) need to fix things for her daughter. In listening to how she described her daughter, it sounded to me as though her daughter was a Red. My client had come up with a grandiose gesture of love and was considering driving across two states to get to her daughter's doorstep by Mother's Day morning and knock on her door and say, "Surprise! I'm here! Will you talk to me now?"

As a coach, I prefer to educate and then turn the decision over to where it needs to be—with the client. So, I simply said, "I wonder if your daughter is a Red Personality Color Style? It was just enough to get my client to immediately ask, "What's a Red Personality Color Style?"

After a brief 30-second explanation of Reds, I also said that I wondered if maybe she (the mother) was a Blue, giving her a brief explanation of a Blue.

She was amazed that I had so accurately described both of their personality styles, and there was a significant shift in her pain level in that moment. It was palpable.

Moving her forward, I suggested she "dial-in" her daughter's Red communication preferences and then asked her, if she was her daughter, how would she like to be approached regarding this communication breakdown.

Dial-in the other Color Style

She instinctively knew right away that the best method at this point in their relationship was to call and leave a message that she wanted to come to her daughter's city and spend some time visiting, quickly concluding the call by asking her daughter to let her know which date would work best for her?

With a Red you give choices. You never beg for permission. You share your authentic intention, stand firm on it and require an answer to your question.

With such a significant energy shift, and as mothers and their children are energetically connected, the daughter undoubtedly felt her mother's emotional shift from Blue **worry energy** into Red **directive energy.**

Within just two days, the daughter called to just talk. It wasn't even Mother's Day yet. It was at this time that my client gave her daughter several choices about when it would be a good time for her to come for a visit.

Here are the simple steps you can take to shift yourself and others out of relational suffering:

Step 1: Stop, Look, Listen for the Color Styles

Step 2: Offer Color Style Education, "I wonder if ..."

Step 3: Dial-in other person's Color Style language and attitudinal tone for your solution and you put an end to suffering about it.

Step 4: Keep dialed-in on their **Color Style** and you will **Synergize** your relationship.

You can expect to experience a softening of others' defensiveness toward you, and this will be largely due to the fact that you are learning to use Color Style language, attitudinal tone and energy as you start dialing-in the Color Style necessary to communicate effectively.

This **SYNERGIZING** **Transformational Program** prompts you to find answers, and the first question to challenge Frog Speak is:

"What is NOT dealing effectively with people and situations in your life costing you ... in your health, time and energy?"

I can only say I wish I had this information decades earlier than I did. My twenties and early thirties felt like someone running their fingernails down the blackboard of my soul—clearly that's why I did the work to find how to **SYNERGIZE** all 4 Color Styles in my life and be effective and confident in my world so I could help others experience confidence, peace and productivity in all of their relationships in each of the 7 Life Areas.

What would it be worth to you to have every single relationship in your life—even the ones that have been impossible—**SYNERGIZED**?

If you feel you need additional coaching as you work on transforming your relationships using Color Style Synergy, you will find a current list of Certified Facilitators and Coaches available to work with you at the website listed in the program information pages at the end of this book.

If you are seeking the need for additional clarity as you start applying the Color Styles to your friends, co-workers and family, whether through home-study audio/video programs or in-person events, the website will help you find one of the ways that will be right for you.

**'All colors are friends
of their neighbors
and the lover of their opposites.'**

-Marc Chagall

Now, if you haven't already done so, I want you to get out there and take the **Personality Style Profile** test o see what Color you are. Be a TurnAround Specialist and, with this information, go

Make A Positive Difference!

The search for truth...

is like standing at a ten-foot-high, solid wooden fence. It's too long to get around and too high to climb, so our only option is to find some little knothole in the fence, poke our eyeball in, and see what we can see.

Now on the other side of the fence is a cow. Some people look through the hole and see a horn and they say, "Ah, the horn is the truth." Others look through and see the beautiful brown skin and say, "Ah, brown must be truth." Then others look through and see the tail swishing back and forth and are convinced that the ever-moving tail is the way.

While they all see part of the picture, no one person can see it all.

- author unknown

About The Publisher

As a TurnAround Specialist and MasterMinding Maven®, Mary Robinson Reynolds founded **Heart Productions and Publishing** in 1990, to build on her success as an educator, coach, consultant, entrepreneur, speaker and author.

Heart Productions & Publishing creates and markets inspirational products that meet the needs of all people wanting to heal their lives in areas of relationships, time, health and money.

Since its inception, Mary's primary interest has been to lift and elevate people working on the matters of the heart. So our goal, like our name, is to heal people's minds and hearts, and to renew their spirits.

If you have enjoyed this book and wish to learn more about our flash online movies and our full line of beautifully designed products and resources that really do make a difference, please visit us at:

MakeADifference.com

About The Author

Mary Robinson Reynolds paid her way through college as frozen foods stocker and grocery check-out clerk, long before scanners! Over the past thirty years, Mary has lead a very diverse and interesting life as a waitress, grocery store clerk, teacher, coach, counselor, consultant, trainer, network marketer and an 18-wheel long-haul "refer" team truck driver delivering produce, fresh and frozen products to food distribution warehouses nation-wide!

Today, Mary is the Author and Producer of the world renowned Internet videos, **MakeADifferenceMovie.com** and **AcknowledgmentMovie.com** — amassing over 10 million views within a few short months of their releases.

She has written eight books and has spoken to tens of thousands of people in a two-year period in every major city in the U.S. As a professional speaker, Mary's dynamic presentation range covers the spectrum from subtle, lightly spiritual and endearing to outrageously, side-splittingly funny, to hammer-the-point intensity. She is also wise, humorous and masterful at helping others trust that what they prefer is valid.

As an author, she writes as she speaks, with vocabulary that's familiar and engaging. As a consultant, her advice is direct, not airy-fairy encouragement, to get people going with the changes they know they need to make. She opens your "heart" with gentle, probing questions like, "So how do you really prefer it to be?" and "Why do you think you can't have it?"

Mary spent her early professional years as a K-8 classroom teacher and then as a K-12 counselor. She was having tremendous, measurable academic results with the kids nobody else wanted in their classrooms and developing "attitudinal" energy techniques to empower students and parents to bridge effective communication and leadership within the educational system.

As a former girls volleyball and basketball coach who won championships in each sport, she knows what it takes to energize and positively influence teams to winning outcomes with synergistic focus and intention.

She parlayed her phenomenal success with at-risk youth into Continuing Education Courses for Portland State University on how to be energetically effective educators. For the past two decades, she has taken her exceptional programs to educational professionals, business leaders, entrepreneurs, corporate managers and administrative assistants conducting training and consulting on how to be effective in creating improvement in their organizations through the power of Team Synergy.

During this same time period, she was also an active network marketing business builder in *The People's Network* (TPN)—a Positive Television company. Known as "The Success Channel," it was one of the most revolutionary concepts ever introduced to the television industry. During the first two years of building this business, her organization's exponential efforts brought in well over 1200 business associates, and Mary was recognized as one of TPN's Top 50 Producers. When TPN merged with Pre-Paid Legal, Inc., she put all of her efforts into raising her family while systematically building her publishing and production company.

She has first-hand knowledge of the day-to-day demands of owning and running a business - customer service, recruiting, training, managing - as well as the long term goals of group development - contracts, negotiations, sales, branding, production costs, increasing customer base.

As a TurnAround Specialist, Mary knows that running a business also includes effectively dealing with negative mindsets and misunderstandings that can lead to contagious gossip and de-energizing back-stabbing among staff, which can —if not effectively defused—ultimately seep out to consumers and business associates. The development of her work with such a diverse and creative group of individuals has been key to the growth and reach of her business to make a difference.

Keep Your Momentum Going!

*21st Century Transformational Leaders know
that training is most effective when viewed (and conducted)
as an ongoing process rather than a one-time event.*

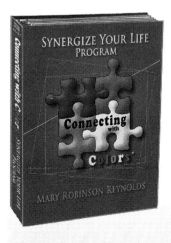

**Connecting with Colors®:
SYNERGIZE Your Life**
Put your knowledge of
the 4 Personality Styles
to work for you!
Video/Audio Program
plus Workbook

A 7-Session Program that Includes all the Areas
of Your Life— a companion to the
Connecting with Colors® Book.

You CAN Make it Happen! Transform problematic personal relationships for
the better with this Electronically Downloadable Video & Audio Program for
Audio MP3s, Video plus Workbook you can study at your own pace.

Dissolve the barriers when you understand the 4 Color Styles. Put an end to
de-energizing communication **NOW** as you positively transform conversations
in all areas of interests:

•Work	•Home	•Management	•Sales
•Love/Sex/Money	•Parenting/Teaching	•'Tweens/Teens	

Positive Transformation!

With the **Connecting with Colors®: SYNERGIZE Your Life** Video/ Audio Program, Mary will show you exactly what you can do to transform difficult people and situations in 30 seconds or less as you come to understand personality styles and the New Science as it relates to Attitudinal Energy.

Mary takes you through the 4 Color Personality Styles step-by-step as they relate to each of the 7 important areas of our lives. This is the kind of information that is self-sustaining and amazingly long lasting. To learn how to create productive 2-Way Communication, you will want to have this information well in hand. (This program includes Complimentary Access to ALL 7 Personality Style Profiles–PSPs!)

Connection Turns ME Into WE = Synergy
Wristbands in Four Colors

What you will truly enjoy about Mary's Program is that you will learn how to shift quickly out of any and all relational suffering in each of the 7 Life Areas! You will actually feel RELIEF about those problematic areas of your own personality style. You will learn that your strengths, ironically because they are strong, are sometimes also your problematic areas. But you won't be left wondering what to do about it. To Learn More go to:

ConnectingWithColors.com/Program

We Also Recommend.....

Academic Success 101:
Online Course for Educational Professionals & Parents

Companion book to this training is *Make A Difference with the Power of Connection* Gift Book & DVD.

Because Mary's professional training career started in education—she had unprecedented success with at-risk students—she developed this 15-hour training to Make A Difference in how we are training teachers and parents.

Discover how to "think" about what's really going on in unproductive and intense behavioral and academic situations. (Training includes 1 session for *Connecting with Colors.*)

To Learn More go to: AcademicSuccess101.com

Coaching with Color Styles UCoach Program
Created by Coach Mary Schrad & Coach Mary Reynolds

Create Winning TEAM Synergy by InteGREATing Your Team's Personality Styles: a program that gets the 4 predominate personality styles working together to WIN! Learn the how to process of improving communication as a lifelong practice.

By integreating, you will become more in tune with a variety of gains. These new skills go beyond the court!

To Learn More go to:
TeamIntegreat.com

And Other Empowering Programs...

Make A Difference with the Power of Acknowledgment

A series of UTRAIN™ Programs that include 6 Electronically Deliverable Short Movies.

A super-sized comprehensive, cost-effective, Do-It-Yourself Training Program to bring to your entire organization with daily activities and easy to implement outlines. Programs for: Business, Education, Organizations and Churches.

The foundation for this program is that it takes 30 days to integrate a new habit. Therefore, in order to impact positively the culture of an organization, engaging leaders need to commit to utilizing Mary's activities in staff meetings and trainings. The activities that are designed for this program directly gently and yet powerfully address the Social Emotional Issues surrounding self-esteem, to create an energized and uplifted corporate culture. (Training includes 1 session for *Connecting with Colors*.)

To Learn More go to: MakeADifference.com/Acknowledgment

Stay Married: Make More Love, Less Conflict

Home Study Online Course

Do you believe it will take a miracle to save your marriage? Well, understand this: It's not over . . . unless you decide it's over! This course teaches that the effects of love are maximal and natural in the presence of love. If and when we find our spiritual center, a miracle will automatically occur. Thought is the level of cause, and the world is the level of effects.

Our greatest power to heal our marriages is our power to think about it differently. Our greatest hope lies not in "over-powering" reactions like shaming, blaming and condemning...but in our power to transform consciousness. Statistics tell us that half of all marriages end in divorce, and the percentage is even higher in second marriages. As a society we are able to leave marriages more easily today, but Mary covers what it will take to learn how to stay married and make more love and have less conflict in this *Home Study Online Course*. (Training includes 1 session for *Connecting with Color*.)

To Learn More go to: Stay-Married.com

How to Become Certified in

Connecting with Colors® - CWC Facilitator Training

Becoming a **Connecting with Colors® Certified Facilitator** is an exciting and dynamic process that can take place on or off site, depending on the number of people you want to train. Larger companies often prefer to hold training workshops on-site for maximum value.

For smaller organizations or for those who desire to train key people, Mary conducts regional open enrollment Facilitator Certification Trainings.

Enhance your training department programs and help achieve new levels of success for all in your organization! Schedule a Certified Facilitator workshop!

My Thing + Your Thing = A Beautiful Thing!

OPEN DOORs with my **FUN EDU-TAINMENT** of the Color Personality Styles then, if you want, you can move more easily into my companion products or your own, along with services that complement Your Thing.

Licenses You to Train anywhere you market. You keep 100% of the revenue you earn from your Speaking / Training Engagements & 40% commissions on companion products sales.

As a Mary Reynolds *Connecting with Colors® Personality Style & Team SYNERGY™* Certified Facilitator, you can learn exciting techniques that help unite people in a common goal. Gain powerful skills that will help you communicate more effectively with others. Discover ways to improve professional and personal relationships in every important Life Area.

For more information on how Mary Robinson Reynolds can help your organization:

ConnectingWithColors.com/Facilitator

"You gave us the competitive edge we were looking for!"

"I am writing to you today to express my appreciation for such a wonderful seminar that you put on for our employees....In the automotive business, where understanding the customer becomes paramount in all of our departments, your seminar hit the mark. We knew we had to find a way to effectively communicate to our customers to remain profitable in such a competitive atmosphere as the retail automotive business is, and your **Connecting with Colors Training** did just that, in fact Mary, you have given us the competitive edge we were looking for. Thank you."

Daniel J. Morris
Dealer Operations Manager
Dave Hamilton Autodealership

"Mary's techniques are the best I've ever seen!"

I first heard Mary speak about a year ago. I was very impressed with her ability to 'touch' the audience. Her techniques are some of the best I've ever seen and her sincerity is so clear that no one can misconstrue it as being contrived.

As time went by and I made some adjustments in our support center organization structure, I realized we had varying levels of skill when the employees were involved in team oriented situations.

I called Mary. We discussed the kinds of issues I was seeing, and she customized a one-and-a-half day team training session that was delivered in July. It went very well. Mary continues to follow-up and is available if I or the managers have questions.

I highly recommend Mary Reynolds to you. If you have questions, please feel free to contact me!"

Sally Phares
University and Community College Systems of Nevada
System Computing Services

22252895R00069

Printed in Great Britain
by Amazon